YORK'S
HISTORIC
ARCHITECTURE

YORK'S
HISTORIC
ARCHITECTURE

SCOTT D. BUTCHER

Charleston   London

THE
History
PRESS

Published by The History Press
Charleston, SC 29403
www.historypress.net

First published 2008

Manufactured in the United Kingdom

ISBN 978.1.59629.503.2

Library of Congress Cataloging-in-Publication Data

Butcher, Scott D.
York's historic architecture / Scott D. Butcher.
p. cm.
Includes bibliographical references and index.
ISBN 978-1-59629-503-2 (alk. paper)
1. Architecture--Pennsylvania--York--Guidebooks. 2. Historic buildings--Pennsylvania--
York--Guidebooks. 3. York (Pa.)--Buildings, structures, etc.--Guidebooks. 4. York (Pa.)--
Guidebooks. I. Title.
NA735.Y67B88 2008
720.9748'41--dc22
                                    2008018155

In loving memory of my grandfather, Laverne J. Butcher (Gramps), who always enjoyed hearing about whatever local history project I happened to be working on.

CONTENTS

ACKNOWLEDGEMENTS

Much of the research for this book was conducted using Historic York, Inc.'s library, and I am grateful to Karen Arnold and Mindy Higgins for their assistance and support over the years. Further research was conducted using the Library and Archives of the York County Heritage Trust. The genesis of this book was the website www.virtualyork.com, which garnered far more interest and hits than I could have ever imagined. From the time the site was first launched until the publication of this book, I spoke with many people about many different buildings throughout the county. I am indebted to everyone who provided advice or pointed me in the right direction. I'm sure I've forgotten as many as I have remembered, but some of those who helped me along the way include: Jim McClure, Richard Banz, June Lloyd, Lila Fourhman-Shaull, Richard Ward, Frank Dittenhafer, David McIlnay, Polly Stetler, Paul Doutrich, Scott Royer, Brad Smith, Ken Oatman, Georg Sheets, Fran Keller, Gene Schenck, Gordon Freireich, Carol Kauffman, Frank Countess, Kirsten Stauffer, Tom Brandt and all those I've failed to mention.

INTRODUCTION

When one thinks about American architecture, various towns and images immediately come to mind. The iconic institutions of Washington, D.C. The brownstones of New York City. The futuristic skyline of Seattle. Some might associate American architecture with such well-known architects as Frank Lloyd Wright, Henry Hobson Richardson or even Thomas Jefferson.

Few people, however, would ever immediately think of York, Pennsylvania. But the 5.3-square-mile city of York has more to offer than one might think.

In central Pennsylvania, we are blessed with something that much of the remainder of the United States is not: a rich architectural heritage. Why is that? First of all, our collective history predates the American Revolution. Second, we've been leaders of business and industry since the 1700s. Third, and perhaps most important, we are kind of stubborn, slow to change. While this may not always be a good thing, in the case of architecture, this character trait has helped preserve many central Pennsylvania communities from the wrecking ball of development.

One great example of this architectural heritage is York, which is a microcosm of historic American architecture and an open-air gallery of diverse styles. In the 1720s, the European settlers began arriving in what is today York County. Germans settled in the Kreutz Creek Valley just west of the Susquehanna River and the Pigeon Hills in the southwestern portion of the county. Scots-Irish settlers migrated toward the southeastern section of the county, while English Quakers settled in northwestern York County. Some of the earliest buildings still remain, including the Johannes and Cristina Schultz House, Martin Schultz House and Dritt Mansion. Western travelers followed an old Native American trail, the Monocacy Road. At the point where the trail crossed the Codorus Creek, a town was established in

The picturesque York City Market House was constructed in 1878 and designed by J.A. Dempwolf in the High Victorian Gothic style.

1741. York Town, as it was called, was laid out by Thomas Cookson, who used a checkerboard grid of streets based upon the design of Philadelphia.

Early buildings were predominately German in style, with asymmetrical construction, central chimneys and half-timbers. One of the first buildings constructed in town was the Martin Eichelberger home and tavern, which still stands today and is better known as the Golden Plough Tavern. The half-timber construction is straight out of the German Black Forest and is the last of a style that used to be common in central Pennsylvania. Some early buildings were constructed in the more formal Georgian style; after all, Penn's Woods was settled by the English. The 1754 courthouse no longer stands, but the Joseph Chambers House, better known as the Gates House, still exists, as does the Willis House and Friends Meeting House. The Georgian style focused on symmetry and balance; while the Germans preferred central chimneys, the English preferred end chimneys. York's Georgian buildings were less elaborate than those being constructed in the larger towns like Philadelphia.

York Town was in many ways a frontier town, laid out seventeen years before Pittsburgh was founded. Originally part of Lancaster County, York

The York County Jail was constructed in 1854 adjacent to the almshouse. The Norman-influenced castle was designed by Edward Haviland.

became its own county in 1749. Adams County to the west was part of York County until 1800.

In 1777, as the British army advanced toward Philadelphia, the Second Continental Congress fled westward, regrouping for one day in Lancaster. They agreed to proceed farther west, beyond the safety of the Susquehanna River. In York Town they reconvened, creating a clash of cultures. York was a small town where most inhabitants spoke German. The delegates of the Continental Congress were wealthy men, accustomed to a vastly different lifestyle. But here they would stay, governing the fledging nation for nine months. The first national day of Thanksgiving was declared in York, and treaties of friendship and alliance with France were ratified. But the single most important task of the Second Continental Congress while in York was the debate and adoption of the Articles of Confederation, precursor of the Constitution.

After Congress returned to Philadelphia, York was in some ways forever changed, no longer a sleepy frontier town. There are over a dozen buildings in the city of York that date from the 1700s, and many more in the surrounding areas. Several of these buildings are operated by the York County Heritage Trust and are regularly open for tours. These include the

Known as the York County Almshouse or Poorhouse, the original buildings were constructed in 1805, with this hospital building completed in 1828.

Golden Plough Tavern, Horatio Gates House and replica of the Colonial Court House, where the Second Continental Congress met.

As the new nation grew, so did York. Westward expansion continued, and York's location made it a hub of activity for travel. Hotels and taverns continued to be built to keep up with the demand. The growing county required more government, and a second building was constructed in Centre Square, adjacent to the courthouse. This building was known as the State House, and was the location of the county land office as well as storage space for county records. A market shed was also located in the square, providing a location for the sale of fruits, vegetables, breads and other items.

Architecturally, York moved into the Federal era. While York's Georgian buildings were never as elaborate as their urban counterparts, the refined Federal style fit nicely with York's conservative personality. In the early 1800s, many buildings were given Greek Revival features, paralleling the national love of classical architecture as designers and builders looked to the democratic ideals of ancient Greece for inspiration.

Throughout the years, York has defined itself as a colonial town; in fact, "Colonial York" was once used to market the area to tourists. However, in architectural terms, "Victorian York" is far more appropriate. Pennsylvania Dutch ingenuity turned into industrial innovation as the Industrial Revolution took hold in America. The first coal-burning locomotive was built in York, as was the first iron steamboat. Local industrialists began acquiring wealth, and higher-style buildings soon began appearing in town and throughout the county.

By the time the Civil War erupted, York was a thriving community of 8,600 people, with York County home to over 62,000 residents. Buildings were taller and grander, such as the six-story Hartman Building, Classical Revival Second York County Court House and classically influenced York County Almshouse. York was a regional center of commerce. The railroad had arrived in 1838, allowing local businesses to flourish. Companies like the Pennsylvania Agricultural Works, P.A. & S. Small and Billmeyer & Small Co. were sending products far and wide. York County, however, was still very much an agrarian community.

It was this combination of commerce, transportation, location and agriculture that made York an attractive target for the Army of Northern Virginia, which arrived in the county in late June 1863. York became the largest Northern town to be occupied by the Confederate army during the Civil War. A skirmish erupted in Wrightsville as the Pennsylvania militia burned the longest covered bridge in the world, which spanned the Susquehanna River between York and Lancaster Counties, to halt the Confederate advance. And in southwestern York County, the Battle of Hanover began when the Union and Confederate cavalries met unexpectedly on the streets of the York County borough. By the end of the month, over thirty thousand Confederate soldiers were either in or heading toward York County. Newly appointed head of the Army of the Potomac General George Meade sent several telegraphs stating that he was planning to proceed to Hanover and Hanover Junction. Had this happened, the two armies may very well have fought in York; however, Meade redirected his army, and the Confederates massed near Gettysburg instead.

York's leaders had agreed to offer no resistance in turn for the town being spared. This decision may have been controversial; however, it may very well have preserved York's rich architectural heritage. No buildings were destroyed during the Confederate occupation.

Victorian architecture began appearing on the streets of York after the Civil War. Italianate mansions were constructed by many of York's wealthy, and the Second Empire row home became a staple of York's streetscape. Churches embraced both Gothic and Romanesque traditions in their buildings, and many added Victorian touches to the façades. High Victorian buildings like the York City Market, York Collegiate Institute,

York Post Office and Central Market House were constructed, showcasing community pride. Streetcars began providing public transportation, and new "suburban-style" neighborhoods like the Avenues began to attract families away from the downtown.

It was during this period that York's most prominent architect began to make his mark on the city. John Augustus Dempwolf, along with his brother, Reinhardt, designed many of the county's most notable buildings. His firm became a training ground for other architects who would eventually strike out on their own and design York's buildings well into the mid-1900s.

Heading into the twentieth century, York continued to prosper as a regional center for manufacturing, business and transportation. Carriage companies reinvented themselves as automobile makers, and York became a regional center for production, even earning the nickname "Detroit East" for a short period of time. Large department stores such as Bear's, Wiests and Bon-Ton rose in and around Centre Square. The downtown became a center of culture, too, with the York Opera House, Coliseum Ballroom and Capital Theater offering vaudeville, theater and eventually moving pictures. Outward expansion continued too, as the Springdale neighborhood took shape south of the downtown while the Elmwood neighborhood grew beyond the eastern city limits.

As the twentieth century progressed, York's architects continued to follow national trends. Neoclassical buildings—based upon Greek and Roman precedents—were popular for government structures, like the York Post Office on South George Street. Beaux-Arts Classicism, imported from France, found its way into the cityscape, as did Art Deco.

If there is one particular style of architecture that has come to symbolize York, it would be Colonial Revival. Based upon Georgian and Federal architecture—but larger and frequently more elaborate—Colonial Revival buildings are found throughout the city and suburbs. In fact, many new homes and office buildings today are constructed in this style, now more accurately termed "Neo-Colonial" to reflect another resurgence of the style. The Martin Library on East Market Street, designed by Frederick Dempwolf—the son of J.A. Dempwolf—was constructed in 1935 in this style. York City Hall, also designed by Frederick Dempwolf (with architect Robert Stair), is primarily Colonial Revival in style, though it features an impressive Neoclassical entrance. It is said that the lobby was modeled after Philadelphia's Independence Hall and the cupola was built in homage to the one that sat atop the original York County Court House.

York's growth and prominence continued through the 1950s. Soon, however, things changed. Like cities throughout the nation, York began to witness a decline in population as families moved to the suburbs. A ring of population grew around the city. After the families moved, the retailers followed. And those that remained soon fell upon hard times. Stores closed. Theaters darkened. Buildings soon began to suffer from neglect.

But what goes around comes around. York frequently bills itself as a city of revolutions. During the American Revolution, York briefly served as the capital of the young nation. And during the "second" American Revolution (the Civil War), York provided thousands of soldiers and unwillingly hosted the Confederate army. Revolution returned to York in the form of the Industrial Revolution, with York creations including everything from automobiles to pottery to "York"-branded products: York Peppermint Patties, York Air Conditioners, York Barbells and York Imperial Apples. Today, York is in the midst of another revolution: the city is experiencing a rebirth, of sorts, with major new construction and adaptive reuse projects taking place.

In York City, historic buildings are found on every street, around every corner. The York Historic District, as listed on the National Register of Historic Places, encompasses 7,140 acres and over 3,000 buildings throughout much of the downtown. Several other historic districts are located within city limits, including the Springdale, Fairmount and Northwest York Historic Districts. And York County is home to well over 10,000 buildings listed on the National Register of Historic Places, with charming historic communities like Hanover, Spring Grove, Red Lion and Shrewsbury dotting the rolling hills of central Pennsylvania.

The story of York's architecture is in many ways the story of America's architecture, told through the eyes of a small town. There are many towns and cities throughout the country that have a rich architectural heritage, yet few have the diversity of architectural styles that one can find within a few blocks of Continental Square.

CONTINENTAL SQUARE

Continental Square has been the heart of York City since the town was laid out in 1741. From 1750 through 1855, the York County Court House was located in the middle of what was then known as Centre Square. It was from this location that the Second Continental Congress governed the fledging United States of America. In 1793 a second building, known as the State House, was built adjacent to the courthouse. It was smaller in stature, but designed with a higher aesthetic. In 1755, the lieutenant governor of Pennsylvania granted a charter for Wednesday and Saturday markets to take place in Centre Square, a tradition that continued into the late nineteenth century. After the first courthouse and adjacent State House were demolished in 1841, a new market shed was constructed. In 1844, a second shed was built, complete with police headquarters and lockup underneath. Following over forty years of service, however, the sheds were deemed an impediment to traffic. On June 30, 1886, twenty men, seven mules and three horses demolished the sheds, beginning at 2:00 a.m. to avoid protestors.

It was also in Centre Square that the Confederate army, under the direction of General Jubal Early, seized the town and took down a massive U.S. flag, making York the largest town to fall to the Rebel army during the Civil War. In the 1920s, the name was changed from Centre Square to Continental Square to celebrate York's important role as host to the Continental Congress.

Southeast Quadrant

The building at 2 East Market Street is known both as the Golden Swan Tavern and the Weiser Building. It was constructed around 1800 and is one

of the older buildings in York City. Benjamin Hersh originally constructed the building as a tavern. Samuel Weiser opened a dry goods store in 1808 and was best known as a maker of hats, particularly during the War of 1812. Later, the building housed a tin store owned by Ludwig Michael. During the American Revolution, the building that occupied this site served as a depository for weapons, including flintlock muskets and rifles. The Golden Swan Tavern is Federal in style and features a gable roof, end chimneys, double belt course and water table. Note the liberal use of windows, something that distinguishes the Federal style from Georgian architecture. There are also typically more lights (panes) in Federal-period windows when compared to their predecessors. In this case, the first-story windows are twelve over twelve panes, while the upper-story windows are eight over twelve panes. The windows provided both day lighting and natural ventilation for the building's occupants.

The building at 1 South George Street, most recently known as the Futer Bros. Building, was built in 1846 and was originally six stories in height. The lot upon which it stands was created when the town was laid out in 1741. During the American Revolution, the building on this site was a hotel. In 1819, the Sign of General Jackson Hotel opened. Five years later, John Hartman, a local merchant, purchased the property. After William C. Goodridge (see the Goodridge House on East Philadelphia

Street) constructed York's then-tallest building on the northwest quadrant of Continental Square, Hartman decided to build an even taller building. Local legend portrays Hartman as someone who was jealous that an African American had constructed such a tall building, and set out to one-up him. The reality, however, is that Hartman and Goodridge had business dealings, and Goodridge's sons eventually relocated their photography studio into Hartman's building. A seventh story was added in the early twentieth century. The upper floors fell into a state of disrepair and were removed in the 1960s when a new aluminum façade was installed. In 2008, workers removed the siding, revealing the original bricks and keystones that had been hidden for over forty years.

Southwest Quadrant

The Colonial Hotel at 18 South George Street has dominated the square since 1893. When it first opened, the hotel offered seventy-five guest rooms. A 1908 addition expanded capacity to two hundred guest rooms. The dark brick building with sandstone trim was designed in the Chateauesque style; however, a 1947 fire destroyed part of the original mansard roof and conical turret roof. The Chateauesque style found its inspiration in the French chateaux constructed in the sixteenth century. When the building served as a hotel, a dining room was located on the top floor. The south side of the building features a Dempwolf signature block with the year 1908 to signify the date of the building addition.

Next door stands the Rupp (or Rupp-Schmidt) Building at 2 West Market Street. While this tall, narrow building nicely complements the adjacent Colonial Hotel, it is Victorian Romanesque in style. Unique to Romanesque structures downtown, the Rupp Building incorporates golden brick into its façade and is topped with a mansard roof. The northeast corner of the building features the head of a bear above a shield bearing the building's construction date of 1892.

The southwest quadrant of Continental Square was once known as Tyler's Corner. James Smith, York's signer of the Declaration of Independence, maintained an office just off the quadrant on South George Street. While the Continental Congress met in York, Smith's office housed the Committee on Foreign Affairs. A hotel located here, the Globe Inn, played host to many notable early nineteenth-century guests, including the Marquis de Lafayette. Later, a tailor opened a store on this quadrant, employing a young man by the name of Isaac Singer, inventor of the Singer sewing machine.

Northeast Quadrant

The most prominent building on the northeast quadrant of Continental Square is the First National Bank Building at 1 North George Street. Constructed in 1924 utilizing Indiana limestone, the building is an example of Beaux-Arts Classicism. The bank was organized in 1864, and the building's cornerstone contains the year of construction and the year the bank was organized. Original capital was $300,000, and First National Bank was the sixty-seventh national bank chartered in the United States.

The balustraded roof, paired and fluted pilasters and eagle ornamentation help establish the building as Beaux-Arts, though the eagle with spread wings is also reminiscent of Egyptian Revival architecture that sometimes featured a vulture and sun disk with spread wings. Beaux-Arts Classicism is named for the École des Beaux-Arts (School of Fine Arts) in Paris. Many American architects studied there, learning about centuries of European architecture that would influence their designs when they returned home.

The reflective building at 2 East Market Street is somewhat out of place in York's historic downtown, though its highly reflective surface does capture several historic buildings from different angles. Architecturally, the building is considered High Tech, though it is a very simplified interpretation of the style.

In the eighteenth century, Archibald McClean resided in a house on this quadrant. McClean was a surveyor of the Mason-Dixon line as well as a patriot of the young nation. When the Second Continental Congress arrived, his house became the U.S. Treasury. Both the treasurer of the United States and the president of the Board of Treasury stayed here. Despite the dark times that surrounded Congress during most of their stay in York, they did receive good news from Benjamin Franklin, who was overseas lobbying to gain the support of the French government. After the French signed treaties of friendship and alliance—and provided much-needed financial support— the money they contributed is believed to have been brought by wagon to

York and housed in a cellar vault in this building. Currency printed locally, as well as a substantial amount of silver that Congress brought with them to York, was also stored here.

Northwest Quadrant

The buildings on the northwest quadrant of Continental Square are still known to many longtime York residents as "Bear's," named for the former Bear's Department Store that was located here for almost one hundred years. In 1888, Charles H. Bear opened a store in a two-and-a-half-story building on this site. J.A. Dempwolf was hired in 1911 to design an "addition" to the building, with the end result essentially being a totally new structure incorporating a few of the original walls. One year later, Bear's was the first local department store to use motor-driven delivery trucks. Over the years, Bear's continued to expand, eventually acquiring and expanding into adjacent properties. Like many downtown merchants, Bear's saw much of its customer base dissolve in the 1960s as shoppers flocked to suburban shopping centers and malls. In 1975, Bear's was sold to another department store, only to permanently close a few years later. The building at 1 West Market Street is in the Commercial style, though it also includes Italianate-

style brackets for ornamentation. Dempwolf was able to experiment with the Commercial style, as he also designed the Bon-Ton Building on West Market Street during the same period. This style is sometimes referred to as Chicago style, named for the Chicago department stores that launched the design movement, which is characterized by a "skeletal" appearance created by large windows that allow massive amounts of daylight to penetrate deep into interior spaces.

William Goodridge, a free slave and prominent local businessman from the 1820s through 1850s, constructed York's first five-story building (four stories plus usable attic) on this quadrant in the mid-1800s. It was in a top-floor studio that his sons began their pioneering photography work. The building was also a station on the Underground Railroad and is believed to have been the hiding place of Osborne Perry Anderson, an African American who participated in John Brown's raid on Harpers Ferry.

EAST MARKET STREET

York Trust Company

21 East Market Street

The York Trust, Real Estate, and Deposit Company was organized in 1890 with an original capital of $150,000. In 1901, its name was changed to York Trust Company, and in 1910 the company constructed this building from a design by J.A. and Reinhardt Dempwolf. The company grew until 1960, when it merged with the York National Bank & Trust Co. to form the York Bank and Trust Company.

The façade is Neoclassical in style, defined by rustication, a prominent pediment with modillions and colossal Ionic columns. The façade incorporates marble as well as a granite base.

York County Court House

28 East Market Street

The York County Court House is easily one of downtown York's most notable structures. This building was the third courthouse to be built in town. The first stood in Continental Square (then known as Centre Square) from 1755 to 1841. A replica of this building, today called the Colonial Court House, is located along the banks of the Codorus Creek on West Market Street. The second courthouse stood on this site from 1841 until 1898. The six colossal granite Ionic columns from the second courthouse were incorporated into this structure, as was much of the foundation, perhaps because a late nineteenth-century project actually began as an expansion to the existing courthouse. After a rear addition was completed, a planned third-story addition to the existing building was abandoned because the foundation could not support the added weight of another story and three domes.

J.A. Dempwolf was the architect for the new building, which was constructed in 1898. The east and west wings were added in 1958, when a renovation/expansion project removed much of the original grandeur of the courthouse. Perhaps the most distinguishing feature of the building is the three Florentine domes that can be seen from miles away. These domes were inspired by the Florence Cathedral in Italy and contain a number of notable features, including both Corinthian and rectangular pilasters, sculptured leaf elements, window pediments, dentil course and—on the main dome—clocks and a cupola. This building is a study in the American Renaissance—a phrase loosely used to describe the turn-of-the-century architectural styles that included Italian Renaissance, Neoclassical Revival and Beaux-Arts Classicism. The Florentine domes are Italian Renaissance, the portico is Neoclassical and the paired pilasters and ornamentation are Beaux-Arts Classicism. In his 1907 book *The History of York County*, historian George Prowell referred to this building as "one of the most ornamental temples of justice in the State of Pennsylvania or anywhere in this country."

In 2006, the building was renovated, receiving new life as the York County Administration Center. The adaptive reuse project converted the former judicial facility into an office building for county government. Many of the historical features were restored in the process, and the end result was a project that received national recognition as the American Public Works Association's "Project of the Year" for 2007 in the historic renovation category.

Yorktowne Hotel

48 East Market Street

The towering Yorktowne Hotel is another gem in York's architectural portfolio. Its history began in 1924, when the chamber of commerce appointed a committee to deal with the lack of adequate hotel facilities within the city. To raise money to build a new hotel, $1,175,000 of stock was sold in the Community Hotel Company of York, Pennsylvania. W.L. Stoddart of New York City was hired to design the hotel. In October 1925, the glitzy new Italian Renaissance hotel opened with 198 guest rooms, each with its own bathroom. Subsequent additions occurred in 1929, 1933 and 1953. The hotel has hosted many distinguished visitors, including presidents. Today, the Roaring Twenties are still alive at the Yorktowne, which is designated as a Historic Hotel of America by the National Trust for Historic Preservation.

Since it opened, the Yorktowne Hotel has defined York's skyline. The building's red brick exterior is trimmed with ornamental terra cotta. Architectural features include a rusticated ground level, round arched windows with keystones and roof balustrade. Another feature common with Italian Renaissance architecture is present here: distinct horizontal divisions, separated by a belt course. In this case, the ground level has its own identity, the next division features two-story arched windows, the next level contains small windows offset by belt courses, the next five floors incorporate a single identity and a belt course separates this division from the top level of the building.

Philip A. Small House

59 East Market Street

Known today as home to the Lafayette Club, this Greek Revival mansion was built by Philip A. Small, a prominent businessman in the mid-1800s. Small was born in 1797 and lived until 1875. He served as president of the York County National Bank and the York Gas Company, was a trustee of the York County Academy and founded the York & Wrightsville Railroad. With his brother Samuel, he owned P.A. & S. Small, which opened in 1833 and was a diversified business. In addition to being a wholesaler and retailer of hardware and groceries, the company also operated several

mills throughout York County. These mills included the Loucks Mill and Codorus Mill, both of which were seized by the Confederate army in 1863. Small was also an active member of the York County Agricultural Society. The building features a prominent Greek entrance with entablature, flat lintels and dentilled cornice. A lantern (a rooftop structure that allows light into the spaces below while assisting with ventilation) sits prominently atop the roof. During the Confederate occupation of 1863, Cassandra Small—Philip's daughter—wrote letters chronicling the events that occurred in the days leading up to the Battle of Gettysburg. Today, the Small House is home to the Lafayette Club, which was organized in 1891 and named for local favorite and Revolutionary War hero the Marquis de Lafayette. The large Tavern Room on the first floor contains a number of beautiful murals on the walls. These murals were painted by Charles X. Carlson and were based upon the works of early nineteenth-century engraver and artist William Wagner.

Zachariah Spangler House

114 East Market Street

Zachariah Spangler was a notable resident of York Town, serving as both sheriff and justice of the peace in the early 1800s. His beautiful home, built in 1780, is primarily Georgian in style and contains many of the architectural features common for the period. The simple doorway incorporates a fanlight as well as a paneled door and keystone. All windows on the first and second floors have keystones. The front façade includes a water table and a double belt course between the first and second stories. The cornice includes dentils, while the two dormers have a Palladian window treatment. Like many Georgian buildings, the brickwork is of the Flemish bond, with alternating headers (short side of brick) and stretchers (long side of brick).

White Rose Motor Club

116 East Market Street

Built in 1949, the White Rose Motor Club was designed in the Art Moderne or Streamline style. The building has a distinct "streamlined" appearance, courtesy of the curved glass and stainless steel. As the architectural style was inspired by automobiles of the day, it is fitting that this motor club building incorporates the style. The White Rose Motors on West King Street is another automobile-oriented building designed in the Art Moderne style. At one point Art Moderne was considered the final phase of Art Deco; however, today it is viewed as a distinct style. Deco buildings are more angular, while Moderne buildings embrace curves.

Judge Robert and Mary Fisher House

124 East Market Street

This building was the home of Judge Robert J. Fisher, who served as president judge from 1851 until 1881. Prior to 1875 he was the only judge for York and Adams Counties. Born in 1806, Judge Fisher is best known as protector of important public documents during the Confederate occupation. General Jubal Early wanted to burn county records stored in the courthouse to retaliate for the actions of Union soldiers in Virginia; however, Fisher appealed to Early's sense of honor and convinced him that to destroy the records would go against an agreement that General John B. Gordon had struck with town leaders on the eve of the Confederate troops' arrival. The gentlemen's agreement was that in turn for York offering no resistance, the Southern soldiers would not destroy the town. Fisher's wife, Mary, led the York response to help the soldiers wounded in the Battle of Gettysburg.

The building was constructed in 1835. At a modest two and a half stories, it is smaller than the buildings to either side of it. Like many other early and mid-nineteenth-century townhouses, the building is essentially a simple Federal structure with a prominent Greek Revival entrance.

York Water Company

130 East Market Street

The York Water Company was organized in 1816, in part to provide water for fighting fires. By 1840 the company was using cast-iron pipes instead of hollowed logs to convey water. Their first reservoir was built in 1848, and the first sand filter plant was constructed in 1899. The most notable feature of this 1929 building is actually on the inside—a 3,800-square-foot ceiling mural. Upon walking through the doorway, visitors are greeted by a 25-foot-high ceiling decorated in Greek, Roman and Christian mythological themes. Known as the *Great Gift of the Creator to Mankind*, the mural was painted by Gustav Keiterer and, among other imagery, features the signs of the Zodiac. A mid-1960s renovation involved installation of a suspension ceiling that not only covered, but also damaged parts of the fresco. Fortunately, a 1996 restoration returned the masterpiece to its original glory.

The marble Neoclassical Revival building interestingly features Egyptian-influenced columns with palm capitals. The dentilled pediment features a decorative tympanum with water-themed low-relief ornamentation. While the building is Neoclassical in inspiration, it was constructed during the time when Art Deco was popular, and the fountain ornamentation was a popular motif with the latter style.

Milton D. Martin House

145 East Market Street

Milton Martin is a Yorker whose name has survived long after his death, thanks to a substantial donation to begin the library that bears his name. Born in 1859, Martin opened the York Spring Carriage Works in 1886 on the site of the present Strand-Capitol Performing Arts Center. The company manufactured light, medium and heavy truck wagons, eventually adding carriages and carts to its product line. In 1897, the company relocated to West York and became known as Martin Carriage Works. At one point the company produced twenty thousand vehicles per year, making it the largest carriage factory in the Eastern United States. Martin Carriage Works also shipped vehicles throughout the world, including England, Germany, South Africa and Australia. After Martin's death in 1912, the company continued operation, producing commercial automobile bodies and even rocket launchers and other wartime equipment.

Milton Martin was an extremely successful businessman and community leader. He founded the Guardian Trust Company on East Market Street and served as its first president. His mansion on East Market Street is a fine urban adaptation of the Chateauesque style. Stepped parapets emerge from through-the-roofline dormers and a mansard roof is present. Golden brick is used for the façade, which features low-relief ornamentation. The Martin Mansion was built in 1900, as was the adjacent Professional Building at 141 East Market. In York, you never know when you are being watched, and such is the case with this building. Note the two prominent grotesques above the entryway as well as the architect's seal (J.A. Dempwolf) inside the entrance vestibule.

Bonham House

152 East Market Street

This Italianate house was constructed in 1840 and enlarged in 1875 after Horace Bonham purchased it. Bonham could trace his family lineage to the Puritans who arrived on the *Mayflower*. He was a lawyer by training and an artist by passion. Born in 1835, Bonham graduated from Lafayette College and studied art in Munich, Boston and Philadelphia. He was appointed as an internal revenue assessor by President Lincoln but devoted much of his life to his love of art. His work was exhibited throughout the region, including in the Cochran Gallery of Art in Washington, D.C.

This home is notable because it stayed in the Bonham family until 1965, at which time it was donated to the Historical Society of York County. Today a house museum operated by the York County Heritage Trust, the Bonham House is regularly open for tours. Rooms are authentically decorated to reflect the different periods in which Bonham family members were residents. The interior features stained-glass windows and parquet floors, while the backyard features beautifully landscaped gardens. This is actually not uncommon for townhouses in York City, as many feature stunning gardens tucked away from passersby along Market Street and other thoroughfares.

David E. Small House

153 East Market Street

David E. Small, a partner in the Billmeyer & Small Co. rail car manufacturer, built this beautiful brownstone Italianate house in the 1860s. Small was a prominent businessman in York in the mid-nineteenth century, serving as president of the York Gas Company, president of the YMCA, founder and president of First National Bank, director of York Hospital and Dispensary and secretary of the Royal Fire Company. In his earlier career he was involved with a family lumber business, H. Small & Sons, before partnering with Charles Billmeyer in 1857.

The brownstone façade with sandstone trim gives the building more of a New York City feel, and is rarely found in York townhouses. The façade has been slightly altered from its original appearance by subsequent repairs. Wide eaves, arched windows with hood molds and keystones and quoins are some of

the Italianate features. Inside, the building contains frescoes painted by Filippo Costagini and Lorenza Scataglia, Italian artists who also painted frescoes in the nearby Billmeyer House but are best known for their work in the U.S. Capitol Building. In the early 1940s the building housed a restaurant, which was one of the first in York to be fully air conditioned. Ownership changed over the years, and today the building is part of the Martin Library.

Martin Library

159 East Market Street

The Colonial Revival Martin Library was constructed in 1935 and has played a major role in the York community ever since. Industrial magnate Milton Martin, who died in 1912, willed $125,000 to start the library, and another $60,000 to create a trust fund for library maintenance. He requested that the library be built near his home on East Market Street; however, more money was required to finance construction, so the funds were invested. In 1920, a lot on the corner of East Market and Queen Streets was purchased. When the library was finally constructed fifteen years later, it opened with a collection of twenty-two thousand books.

The brick building features an Indiana limestone entryway with swan's neck pediment and pineapple finial. Its symmetrical brick façade, hipped roof, cupola, keystones, belt course, urn finials and swags are all Colonial features popular with the stylistic revival. The small oval window in the pediment is known as a bull's-eye window.

First Presbyterian Church

215 East Market Street

In 1762, a small group of English-speaking Presbyterians began meeting in one another's homes. This group evolved into the congregation of First Presbyterian Church. The Penn family owned the land on which the building stands until 1785, at which time it was conveyed for the purpose of establishing a church. Construction on the original building began in 1789. In the 1830s, the Presbyterian congregation split into old and new branches, both of which wanted the property. York County courts determined that the new branch had rights to the church and land.
York's signer of the Declaration of Independence, James Smith, was buried here in 1806, and his grave—marked by an Egyptian obelisk—is still visible from East Market Street.

The current church was constructed in 1860 and is primarily Romanesque Revival in style, though some Italianate features are also present. The mostly monochromatic façade features arched windows with hood molds, arched corbel table and a large central tower. Romanesque Revival was popular for American churches constructed in the second half of the nineteenth century.

John A. Weiser Home

218 East Market Street

The Weiser family constructed this handsome Italianate home in 1875. John A. Weiser was born in 1824 and attended the York County Academy. He worked in his father's dry goods store on the southeast quadrant of Continental Square, eventually taking over the business. The store remained

in the family for three generations, as his sons eventually succeeded him. Weiser was a founder and director of Farmer's National Bank, a director of the York County Bank, president of the York & Gettysburg Turnpike Co. and manager/treasurer of the York & Susquehanna Turnpike Co.

Many Yorkers better know this building as home to the Visiting Nurses Association of York and York County. The organization was founded in 1904 to provide around-the-clock nursing care. The VNA also offered classes for expectant parents and pioneered school nursing locally. They also offered physical therapy, among other services.

The beautiful building exhibits many Italianate features including oriel, wide eaves with brackets, narrow arched windows and foliate lintels. The most striking feature of the façade is perhaps the wrought-iron work on the first floor.

Billmeyer House

225 East Market Street

One of the most elegant Italianate mansions in the area, the Billmeyer House dates from the early 1860s. Charles Billmeyer, original owner of the mansion, began the Billmeyer & Small Co. in 1857 with partner David E. Small, whose mansion is located less than a block away. Billmeyer & Small Co. manufactured rail cars from 1865 to 1902, supplying the Denver & Rio Grande, Mexican National and Mexican Central Railroads, among others.

The house is textbook Italianate, with narrow rounded windows, quoins, wide eaves with brackets, ornate chimney and oriel. A lantern, a type of cupola that exists to let light into spaces below and assist with ventilation, caps the roof. The interior is just as striking, featuring frescoes by Costagini and Scataglia, two Italian artists who assisted in the painting of the U.S. Capitol Building. Today owned by the adjacent First Presbyterian Church, the Billmeyer House is listed on the National Register of Historic Places. The battle to save this building from demolition became a landmark historic preservation case, and is still studied in classrooms throughout the United States.

There are four subtypes of the Italianate style. An Italian villa, typically used for country homes, contains a tower. An Italianate "town house" usually contains a lantern and is more compact than its rural cousin. Another subtype is Commercial Italianate, to which the Hoover Wagon Company building (York Dispatch Newsroom) on East Philadelphia Street belongs. Finally, Italian Renaissance Revival is an outgrowth of the style and is sometimes viewed as the fourth subtype.

Historical Society Museum

250 East Market Street

The Historical Society was formed in 1895, with annual dues of $5. Members originally met on the third floor of the York County Court House. Regular meetings began in 1902, and annual dues were reduced to $2 to increase the membership base. The society worked to raise $2,200 to

start a library. At one point, the organization was located at the Billmeyer House on East Market Street. While the Historical Society was building its membership base, a teacher by the name of J.W. Richley was starting a bicycle business, eventually building an automotive showroom, the J.W. Richley Auto Company, which opened in 1921.

The Historical Society purchased the building in 1958 and renovated it into the Colonial Revival style so prominent throughout the greater York area. A central pediment, door pediment, splayed lintels with keystone, dentil course and water table all create a formal Georgian appearance. On the inside, however, a glimpse of the past remains as the original checkered showroom floor greets visitors in the main hall. Today part of the York County Heritage Trust, the museum houses an impressive collection. Few towns the size of York can boast such a museum, much less the collection of museums that constitute the York County Heritage Trust. Additional properties include the Agricultural and Industrial Museum of York County, Bonham House, Colonial Court House, Fire Museum of York County and Gates House/Plough Tavern/Bobb House complex.

YWCA

320 East Market Street

The York Chapter of the Young Women's Christian Association was established in 1891 and originally met on West King Street. In 1951, the organization constructed this Colonial Revival building for a cost of $650,000, providing accommodations for up to twenty-eight resident girls. Today the YWCA is more active than ever,  spearheading a community renaissance initiative that resulted in the surrounding Olde Town East neighborhood being named the first Elm Street program in the Commonwealth of Pennsylvania.

Colonial Revival is an extremely popular style in York, and this building exhibits many of the typical features: symmetrical façade, fanlight, keystones, dentil course, central pediment with bull's-eye window, hipped roof, belt course and water table.

Asbury United Methodist Church

340 East Market Street

Today, most people think nothing of evening church services. In eighteenth-century York, however, it was believed that evening church services would corrupt the morals of the town's youth. In the late 1790s, the congregation at First Methodist Episcopal Church changed this when they began offering services "at early candle light." The congregation was organized in 1782 and originally met at the site of the present-day Otterbein United Methodist Church on West Philadelphia Street. Their first church building had a fireplace and a dirt floor. In 1820, the congregation incorporated as the First Methodist Episcopal Church in York, and in 1836 relocated to the northwest corner of West Philadelphia and North Beaver Streets. The new church cost $16,000 to construct. By 1850, gas service had been provided to the building. The congregation grew, and in 1873 they constructed a new church for a cost of $24,500. To honor Francis Asbury, the first bishop of the Methodist Church in America who visited York in 1807, the congregation

changed its name to Asbury United Methodist Church in 1968 when it merged with Evangelical United Brethren Church.

In 1925, an education building was constructed at the present site on East Market Street, and the Late Gothic Revival sanctuary building was constructed in 1937. The open lawn in front of the education building is a rarity downtown, where most buildings are not set back from the sidewalk. The unique spire atop the sanctuary building is known as a "fleche," a French word that translates as "arrow."

Goodwill Fire House

835 East Market Street

The Goodwill Fire Company was organized in 1839 in Freystown, an area that is now the eastern part of York City. Originally known as the Springgarden Active Fire Company, they purchased a hand bucket pump engine their first year in operation. In 1852 the company changed its name to Goodwill and purchased a suction pump engine. A new engine house was constructed on East Market Street in 1858, and this firehouse was built in 1894. The station was sold to York City in 1902.

The building is primarily Italianate in style, with a projecting bay window, corbel table, quoins and prominent hood molds over the rounded windows to either side of the garage. Other windows feature splayed lintels with keystones, and the bell tower incorporates paired arched openings in a recessed arch. Perhaps the most notable features are the rusticated first story and high-relief wolf ornamentation—the station mascot—over the arched garage door.

WEST MARKET STREET

Fluhrer Building

17–19 West Market Street

Though certainly not the largest building in York—or even on the first block of West Market Street—the Fluhrer Building is one of the most significant edifices in York. Harry H. Fluhrer established "York's finest jewelry store" (as he called it) in York in 1884; the business was also known for the sale of china and silver. Fluhrer's store prospered, and J.A. Dempwolf was commissioned to design a new building, which was built in 1911. Dempwolf's design included a façade of glazed tile that sparkles during the day, revealing many fine architectural details. The recessed arches on the fourth story

reveal two dates: 1884 (the year the store was founded) and 1911 (the year the building was constructed). On the west side of the building, near the front, is a date stone with "JAD 1911" to signify Dempwolf's involvement. The building is Commercial in style, though it incorporates Italian Renaissance sensitivities.

Trinity United Church of Christ

32 West Market Street

Trinity Reformed Church was built in 1866 by the English branch of the First Reformed Church, which had been organized in 1743 The building was constructed at a cost of $60,000, including organ. In 1905, Theodore Helb, owner of a local brewery, presented a new $7,000 pipe organ to the congregation. In 1957, a narthex was added. The site on which the building stands once belonged to Colonel Thomas Hartley, York's first congressman and a Revolutionary War figure who lived in a house on this site.

Trinity UCC is Romanesque Revival in style, evidenced by the monochromatic appearance, steeple tower, rounded arches and corbel table. Like First Presbyterian Church, this building also contains Italianate features, particularly on the steeple tower. These features include a wide cornice with paired brackets and hood molds. The second tower is shorter, which is a common element with Romanesque Revival churches. The slate roof was quarried in Delta, York County.

National House

53 West Market Street

Known over the years as the White Hall Hotel, National House and Jack's Department Store, this building was one of the largest local hotels for many years. Built on "Dinkel's Corner" in 1828 by Ziba Durkee, the White Hall Hotel was known for its lavish décor. The building was expanded in the early 1860s when the fourth floor, balconies and rooftop observatory were added. The stacked verandas are reminiscent of antebellum Southern architecture. While a hotel, this building played host to many celebrated visitors, including President Van Buren (1839) and Charles Dickens (1842).

In fact, Dickens later wrote that the best beefsteak he had in America was served at this very place. In 1921, the building became home to Jack's, a fashion store that was a favorite shopping destination for many decades. Jack's was founded in 1912 and originally sold both men's and women's clothing, but dropped men's clothing in 1928. The building of today showcases its appearance in 1863, the same year that the Confederate army occupied York.

Bon-Ton Building

100 West Market Street

For several decades this structure was part of a vibrant shopping scene within two blocks of Continental Square and served as the flagship store of the Bon-Ton Department Store chain. While today there are over 275 Bon-Ton stores in the Northeastern United States, the store had humble beginnings. In 1898, Max Grumbacher opened a dry goods store and millinery at 36 West Market Street. Business grew, and in 1911 this building was constructed from a design by J.A. Dempwolf. Its tearoom could hold up to 250 people and was a popular meeting place for Yorkers. By 1921, demand for space required the Bon-Ton to expand into an adjacent building. Air conditioning was added in 1941, and in 1956 York's first "moving stairway" was installed. The store was modernized and renovated multiple times, including removal of one of the building's defining features: the stepped parapets along the roofline. Like many urban retailers throughout the United States, the Bon-Ton eventually decided to close its downtown store in favor of a modern new store in the suburbs.

In 1989, the York County Commissioners undertook an ambitious project to renovate and adaptively reuse the massive empty building for county government offices. The former department store was given a face-lift to emulate its original appearance, though the re-creation of the high-relief ornamentation on the stepped parapets was cost prohibitive. Still, the building of today pays homage to the original Dempwolf design. The façade comprises glazed tile and massive three-part "Chicago" windows. Compare this Commercial-style building to the Bear's Department Store on Continental Square, as well as the nearby Rosenmiller Building. All three buildings were designed by J.A. Dempwolf and demonstrate different applications of the Commercial style.

When the Second Continental Congress met in York, the building that stood on this site housed the Hall & Sellers Printing Press. Originally owned by Benjamin Franklin, the press was used to print American currency as well as the *Pennsylvania Gazette*. Later, Revolutionary War figure Major General John Clark lived in a home on this site.

General Wayne Headquarters Replica

101 West Market Street

The York Bank & Trust Co constructed this building in 1958. Its exterior was designed to replicate the building that stood on this very spot during the American Revolution. In 1781, General "Mad Anthony" Wayne came to York and set up headquarters while awaiting orders to join the Yorktowne campaign. Four of his men were arrested for trivial offenses, like drinking and swearing. Because Wayne had previously been the object of an attempted mutiny, he ordered the executions of the men in Penn Common to use fear as a way to keep his men in line.

The building later became the Indian Queen Hotel. In 1810, eleven leading citizens established the York Bank and acquired the building. The York Bank, which for many years was the oldest local bank, eventually demolished the building, only to later rebuild it to its original specifications. Note the prominent light fixture on the southeast corner, which is the same one that hung on the original building. Architecturally, the building is a simple Georgian structure, though there are more windows present than with the original building.

York County Gas Company

127 West Market Street

The York County Gas Company was founded in 1848 and was chartered by an act of the Pennsylvania General Assembly in 1849. One year later the company received a contract to light the streets of York. This was accomplished via a lamplighter, who had to climb a ladder and individually light each lamp with a match. Eventually it became the duty of policemen to light the lamps. By 1887 electric lights had replaced the gas lamps.

The beautiful building along West Market Street was constructed in 1920 and exhibits many decorative features including wreath festoons, modillions, dentils and foliate brackets. A massive mural, one of over twenty murals found throughout the downtown, adorns the west side of the building. Major murals celebrate York's history and people, while "mini-murals" in Cherry Lane replicate the works of Lewis Miller, a notable nineteenth-century folk artist.

General Horatio Gates House

157 West Market Street

The Gates House stands adjacent to the Golden Plough Tavern, and both buildings are listed on the National Register of Historic Places.

Constructed by Joseph Chambers in 1751, the building is an example of a Pennsylvania Georgian house with balanced stone façade and pent roof.

The building's most notable resident was General Horatio Gates. While the Second Continental Congress was meeting in York Town, Gates led the Continental army to a victory over the British in Saratoga, New York. Subsequently, he was invited to York Town to preside over the Board of War. Because he came with his wife and servants, he was not pleased to stay in an inn. In February 1778, he moved into a former tavern that had been converted into a private residence.

It was during this period that a number of military and political leaders had grown increasingly unhappy with Washington's leadership of the Continental army. Philadelphia was now under British control. This loose-knit group became known as the Conway Cabal, named for Thomas Conway, a French general serving in the Continental army. Conway had penned a letter critical of Washington and dispatched it to the delegates in York Town. Word of the letter spread, and even reached General Washington in Valley Forge. There were other leaders also unhappy with the status of the war, and some believed that Washington should be replaced with General Gates.

Under this backdrop, a young French nobleman and friend of Washington, Marquis de Lafayette, came to York Town to discuss his appointment to command a Canadian campaign against the British. A popular local legend tells of Lafayette saving General Washington's job while in York via the "toast that saved the nation." According to legend, Lafayette was invited to a lavish dinner held at this house in his honor, and then listened as the conspirators—including General Gates—toasted one another but not the commander in chief. Lafayette, disgusted by their intentions, stood and proposed a simple toast to the health of Washington, signifying that he would play no part in the Conway Cabal. There is little factual evidence to support the legend; in fact, immediately afterward, Lafayette wrote of his meeting with the alleged "conspirators," and reported that only one was in disagreement with him. Further, he makes no mention of any toast, dinner or location.

Today, the Gates House—along with the adjacent Golden Plough Tavern—is operated by the York County Heritage Trust and is open for tours.

Golden Plough Tavern

163 West Market Street

Easily one of the most important surviving buildings in York County, the Golden Plough Tavern is also one of the oldest. York was laid out in 1741 at the intersection of the Monocacy Road and the Codorus Creek. That very same year, this building was constructed, literally a stone's throw from the creek. Michael Eichelberger, a prominent German settler, built this building in the German Colonial style. Most likely the tavern was one story at first, and was expanded a few years later. The half-timber appearance is reminiscent of the construction techniques used in the German Black Forest, from where Eichelberger hailed. As a tavern, the building served as an important meeting place as well as an inn for travelers. The first story of the structure comprises hewn logs and chinking infill, while the second story comprises brick and exposed half-timbers in horizontal, vertical and diagonal formation. If you look closely, you'll see the Roman numerals that were used as a construction aid to fit the proper pieces together. The building also contains a solen fenster, or soul window, on the first floor. The purpose of this small opening was to provide the souls of the recently deceased with easy access to the outside, expediting their journey to heaven. Interestingly, the adjacent Gates House did not have a kitchen, meaning that the two distinctly different buildings functioned as one on the interior. This building is open to the public and is operated by the York County Heritage Trust.

Bobb Log House

163 West Market Street

Located to the rear of the General Gates House and Golden Plough Tavern, this simple log house was built in 1811 and was relocated to this site in 1968. Today, it is part of the collection of historic homes and museums operated by the York County Heritage Trust. The building, which is listed on the National Register of Historic Places, is open to the public and provides a glimpse of life in the early 1800s. The house was built by Johann Bernhard (Barnett) Bobb, who was of German descent. While a lot of log houses built during this period were one story with only one or two rooms, the Bobb Log House is notable for its size. Its first floor contains four rooms and a hall, while the second floor is one large open space.

On the south side, the log house exhibits two doors. This design evolved into the "Pennsylvania farmhouse," with one door providing entrance to a hall and the second door providing an entrance directly into the kitchen. In the case of the Bobb Log House, however, the kitchen was probably outside or in a smaller separate structure. The timbers used to construct this building were hewn, or squared, which is why it is considered a log "house." Had the timbers been left rounded and stacked without the chinking, the building would be considered a log "cabin."

York County Colonial Court House

201 West Market Street

The original York County Court House was constructed in 1755 and stood in Centre Square, today known as Continental Square. The structure was renovated in 1815 and torn down in 1841, despite objections from local residents and newspapers. The courthouse would rise again, however, when the York County Bicentennial Commission constructed a replica of the original building in 1976 at the intersection of West Market Street and the Codorus Creek.

During the American Revolution, the Second Continental Congress found haven in York Town, escaping the British troops marching on their home base in Philadelphia. While in York, the Continental Congress debated and adopted the Articles of Confederation, marking the first time the original thirteen colonies formally came together under one central government. It is because of this achievement that York is sometimes referred to as the "First Capital of the United States," though most historians bestow that title on Philadelphia, where the Declaration of Independence was adopted, or even New York City, where the Constitution was adopted and President Washington was inaugurated. Congress also declared the first national day of Thanksgiving in celebration of a Continental army victory over the British in Saratoga, New York, and ratified important treaties with France. During the period that York served as capital of colonial America, General George Washington and his men weathered the brutal winter in Valley Forge. Patriots who served their country in York included John Adams, Sam Adams, John Hancock, John Witherspoon, Thomas Paine, Horatio Gates, Phillip Livingston and Henry Laurens, among others.

The York County Court House is a simple Georgian building with balanced façade, gable roof, dentils, end chimneys, cupola, belt course and water table. The bell that hung in the cupola and called members of Congress to meetings is known as York's Liberty Bell and is on display at the Episcopal Church of St. John the Baptist on North Beaver Street.

The Colonial Court House, Bobb Log House, General Gates House and Golden Plough Tavern all constitute the Colonial Complex of the York County Heritage Trust.

Eli Kirk House

322 West Market Street

Another of York's oldest buildings, this simple Georgian home dates from 1785. Eli Kirk was a prominent clockmaker, active Quaker and president of Vigilant Fire Company, which was originally known as Union Fire Company and was organized in 1780. The tax list of 1783 lists Kirk as a clockmaker with one horse and seven persons. The building is sometimes referred to as the Kirk-Griest House, as Amos Griest was another Quaker who owned the home. He was an active agent working with the Underground Railroad and was known to help

escaped slaves from the Jessop Farm south of York (Apple Hill) to a hiding place in his home, and then move them toward the Susquehanna River.

The Eli Kirk House features a pedimented entrance, Flemish bond brickwork, water table and double belt course.

Market & Penn Farmers' Market

380 West Market Street

York's oldest farmers' market was organized in 1866 to serve the growing populace west of the Codorus Creek. A new building was constructed, and enlarged twice in subsequent years. An 1890 project involved construction of a large "false front" to unify the front façade and connect the two buildings that constituted the market. While the 300 and 400 blocks of West Market Street have seen many changes—from prosperity to decline and back to prosperity—the Farmers' Market has been a consistent presence and withstood the test of time. Today, the market is still home to vendors selling fresh produce, meats, Pennsylvania Dutch specialties and crafts.

This building is listed on the National Register of Historic Places. Notable architectural features include rose windows, fanlights above each of the five entrances, pilasters and brick hold molds. Note the entrances on the far left and far right, which both exhibit a Palladian motif.

Union Lutheran Church

408 West Market Street

Hailed by some local historians as the best stone structure in York, Union Lutheran Church was unfortunately the swan song for architect J.A. Dempwolf. It was his last major design commission, and he passed away before construction was completed. The congregation of this church was organized in 1859, and their first house of worship was constructed in 1860 at a cost of $5,636. In the late 1880s, a new Romanesque Revival chapel was constructed on nearby South Penn Street. This building still stands today.

The current sanctuary building was built in 1927 and is an example of Late Gothic Revival architecture. The prominent tower offers breathtaking panoramic views of York City. Notable architectural features include a granite façade, tower and pinnacles, dome, rose window and pointed arches. Like many churches of the period, the massive sanctuary interior resembles an inverted ship. Picturesque stained-glass windows were created by the Rudy Art Glass Studio of York under the direction of J. Horace Rudy.

Royal Fire Company

757 West Market Street

The Royal Fire Company was organized in 1901 to serve the west end of York, particularly because of industrial expansion into that area. Land was acquired at the intersection of Carlisle Avenue and West Market Street, and a temporary building was constructed. Construction on a permanent brick building began in 1902, and the new firehouse was dedicated in 1904. Today, the Victorian Romanesque building is home to the Fire Museum of York County, which was founded in 1979 and is now part of the York County Heritage Trust. The museum houses vintage fire trucks, horse-drawn fire carriages and much more.

Architectural details include rounded arches, a hipped roof and a bell tower with truncated hipped roof. Note also the quoins, wide eaves and brackets, which add a bit of Italianate to the building. The prominent lion high-relief ornamentation showcases the company's mascot. An elk is present over the entrance roof—this was not original, but was relocated from Rescue Fire Company. A statue in the yard was relocated from Penn Park. John Hamme and Edward Leber were the architects of the unique building. They had both previously worked for the Dempwolf architectural firm and together designed the Meadowbrook mansion in East York, several residences in Springdale and the George Whitely House near York College.

York Fairgrounds

West Market Street/Carlisle Avenue

In 1765, Thomas Penn (son of William Penn) granted a charter to the citizens of York Town to hold two agricultural fairs per year. These fairs were held at Penn Common and originally lasted for two days. This tradition

lasted until 1815. Less than forty years later, the idea was revived, and the York County Agricultural Society was formed. Fairs began again at Penn Common and a site southeast of King and Queen Streets was acquired for a permanent fairground. Originally seven acres, the fairgrounds eventually grew to fourteen acres. During the Civil War the site became a military base known as Camp Scott. Within days of the firing upon Fort Sumter, six thousand men were mustered into service at the camp.

In 1887, the York County Agricultural Society acquired seventy-three acres of land along West Market Street and Carlisle Avenue. Shortly thereafter, the first fair was held there. Old Main was constructed in 1888 and Horticultural Hall two years later, with B.F. Willis serving as the architect.

While the fairgrounds have been expanded and new buildings constructed, the Victorian buildings remain and continue to play an important part of the annual fair as well as shows and conventions held throughout the year. In fact, the York Fair is recognized as "America's Oldest Fair," and has grown into a ten-day event attracting several hundred thousand visitors every year.

GEORGE STREET

John Fisher House

21 North George Street

In 1761, John Fisher constructed a large brick house just south of this building. Fisher was from Swabia in southern Germany and was the first clockmaker in York. His reputation was as a maker of eight-day clocks, and he was also a musician and painter. During his career, Fisher even constructed a small pipe organ. In the second story of his home he kept a small museum, with such items as a wooden Indian chief head and wooden deer head.

His son, also named John, built this house around 1780. He studied medicine in Lancaster and practiced in York. This building functioned as a home, office and drugstore. Restored in 2004 as a restaurant, a small area of hewn logs, showcasing the building's original appearance, was left exposed in the interior.

Strand-Capitol Performing Arts Center

48–60 North George Street

The Strand-Capitol Performing Arts Center is truly a community gem, both for its contribution to the local arts culture as well as its contribution to the downtown streetscape. The Strand and Capitol are actually two distinct structures, even though they have the appearance of one from the outside. A small dance hall known as the Theatorium was built in 1906 on the southwest corner of George and Philadelphia Streets. It was later renamed the Jackson, and was greatly expanded and remodeled in 1917. In 1925, the prominent Appell family constructed the Strand Theater next door and purchased and remodeled the Jackson, renaming it the Capitol Theater. For much of the past century, the Strand and Capitol Theaters have been the cultural center of York. From vaudeville to silent films to "talking pictures," the center has been a popular gathering place for the greater York area. With the advent of suburban shopping centers and movie houses, the Strand-Capitol suffered as downtown York declined, closing in the mid-1970s. But the community responded, determined to preserve and reinvigorate this priceless resource. Business leaders mobilized, and the citizens of York responded. After a fundraising campaign and extensive renovations, the

performing arts center reopened. It has since been expanded, and the complex now includes several adjacent buildings.

The Capitol Theater is the older of the two, constructed in 1917 from a design by Reinhardt Dempwolf. It is a wonderful Italian Renaissance structure with rusticated street level, pedimented doors and windows, pilasters and balustrade. Next door stands the Strand Theater, with a simple Commercial-style façade that complements the Capitol. As impressive as the complex is on the exterior, the grand interiors are notable for their exquisite and picturesque Italian Renaissance features.

The Valencia

146 North George Street

In 1911 the Coliseum Ballroom opened, giving Yorkers a place to dance and hear popular touring acts. Later renamed the Valencia, the building was known far and wide as one of the best ballrooms in the region and played host to crowds of up to two thousand people. A house band, the Blue Moon Orchestra, was well known, but it was the big-

name performers that drew the crowds: Duke Ellington, Tommy Dorsey, Benny Goodman and even Frank Sinatra.

The original façade was torn down in the early 1930s and replaced with a simple Art Deco exterior. The grand ballroom was restored and reopened in the late 1980s.

Frey & Thomas Hardware/Brooks Building/York Motor Car Co.

230–238 North George Street

These three buildings on the 200 block of North George Street each have a story to tell. The building on the left (230 North George) was home to Frey & Thomas Hardware, a wholesale grain and hardware dealer. It was constructed in 1893 and exhibits some Queen Anne detailing. The building in the center (236 North George Street), known as the Brooks Building, was constructed in 1891 and owned by Edward S. Brooks. It also applies some Queen Anne detailing to a simple commercial structure. Today these two buildings are better known as the Lofts on

George Street, a mixed-use redevelopment with commercial space and loft-style condominiums.

The Commercial-style building on the right side of the photo (238 North George Street) was constructed in 1905 on the site of the former York Carriage Company, which was destroyed in a 1904 fire. The company manufactured carriages, buggies and sleighs. A new building was constructed for the Pullman Motor Car Co., which occupied it until 1917. The "Pullman" name was synonymous with luxury automobiles. One of their first cars had six wheels. During their twelve years of operation, as many as twenty thousand cars were produced. Fewer than thirty are known to still exist, and several of them are part of a permanent transportation display at the Agricultural and Industrial Museum on West Princess Street. After the Pullman Motor Car Co. went out of business, Bell Motor Car Co. and Riess Motor Car Co. occupied the building. The north side of the building features restored advertisements for Pullman Automobiles.

Christ Lutheran Church

29 South George Street

The congregation of Christ Lutheran Church dates from 1733 and is the oldest Lutheran congregation west of the Susquehanna River. In 1741, the heirs of William Penn granted land on South George Street to the congregation; a log church was erected in 1743. By the early 1760s, a new forty- by sixty-five-foot stone church had been constructed onsite. From 1812 to 1814 another new church was constructed at a cost of $18,590. Less than a decade later, English-language services were introduced, and in 1829 lamps were purchased to enable evening services. When the first courthouse was demolished in 1841, the York County Commissioners gave the old town clock to the church, and it was placed on the steeple. A chapel was erected to the rear of the building in 1892 at a cost of $15,000. Local architect J.A. Dempwolf served as the superintendent of the Sunday school for several decades.

Originally known as First Lutheran, the church was built in the Federal style. Members of the Second Continental Congress worshipped with the congregation. Captain Michael Doudel of the York Rifles is buried in the cemetery, along with other men who fought in the American Revolution. In addition to the towering steeple, the arched pedimented doorways and western arcade are notable features, though the arcade was a later addition.

Washington Hall

102 South George Street

Originally known as the Odd Fellows Hall, the Washington Hall was constructed in 1850 in the Greek Revival style. Over the years, it has served many purposes. From the time it opened into the 1880s, it housed York's primary entertainment hall (Washington Hall) on the second floor, playing host to theatrical companies and musical groups. During the Civil War, the building became a hospital when the nearby U.S. Army Hospital at Penn Commons was filled to capacity. Wounded soldiers from the Battles of Antietam and Gettysburg were treated here. It

also served as an armory and quarters for troops who were training at the old York Fairgrounds, which had been converted into Camp Scott by the Union army. In the late 1800s, the Independent Order of Odd Fellows helped establish a library on the first floor. The building even served as an interim county courthouse while a new one was being constructed during the late 1890s.

Architecturally, the building resembles a vertically oriented Greek temple; colossal pilasters with Corinthian capitals, classical cornice and pediment are prominent features.

York Post Office

200 South George Street

The current York County Post Office was constructed in 1912 and expanded in 1940; today, it is perhaps York's finest example of Neoclassical architecture. The building is typical of governmental buildings of its era and was built as a memorial to the Second Continental Congress. The original building was constructed at a cost of $135,000 and designed by James Knox Taylor, supervising architect for the Department of the Treasury. Prior to the creation of the General Services Administration, the Treasury Department oversaw design and construction of many federal buildings. Daniel F. Lafean, a

congressman representing York and Adams Counties, obtained funding for the project. He was also able to appropriate funds for new postal facilities in Hanover and Gettysburg.

The 1940 expansion was completed at a cost of $1 million. The façade is primarily marble with a granite base. A monumental portico features eight double Ionic columns and pediment. The remainder of the façade features pilasters, while a prominent balustrade surrounds the roof.

Saint Mary's Roman Catholic Church

311 South George Street

The Gothic Revival St. Mary's Church has been standing on South George Street since 1884. German Catholics who broke away from St. Patrick's Catholic Church founded the congregation in 1852. Originally, the $30,000 building featured a brick façade. A 1914 renovation gave the façade its current granite exterior. The building has the feel of a European cathedral, particularly with the three symbolic doors across the front façade. The center steeple is 185 feet in height.

In 1920, artist Frederick D. del Henwood was commissioned to paint eight images on the sanctuary ceiling. The images, in a style reminiscent of Michelangelo, depict the life of Mary. Unfortunately, as the years progressed these paintings were covered over and forgotten. A 2002 renovation rediscovered the images, and they have since been restored to their original glory. The three towers are notable features, complete with belfries and pinnacles.

D.E. Stetler Dodge

515 South George Street

In 1914, Daniel E. Stetler started an automotive business in Newberrytown, which he relocated to York in 1921. He became successful in both business and community leadership, serving as president of the Kiwanis Club and director of the York Baseball Club. He also served as president of the Auto Dealers of York County. Toward the end of his career, Stetler was recognized as the oldest Dodge auto dealer in the United States. He constructed this building in 1923, adding Plymouth cars to his dealership in 1937 and constructing a service building eight years later.

Today the former showroom is home to the Susan P. Byrnes Health Education Center, a nonprofit organization that was established in 1995 to promote education for healthier living. The organization restored the building, and today the preserved showroom provides a unique backdrop for meetings and special events.

Dempwolf House

701 South George Street

The residence of John Augustus Dempwolf is a visual delight for those who take the time to study the ornamental façade. The Queen Anne home was built in 1886, evidenced by a decorative date stone with low relief present on the second story of the building. The gable facing South George Street is rich with low-relief ornamentation, including an apparent reference to "Old Man Winter."

J.A. Dempwolf was born on October 3, 1848, in Brunswick, Germany. He had six siblings, including Reinhardt—who would later join the Dempwolf architectural practice—and Charles, founder of York Chemical Works. Early in his career, J.A. Dempwolf worked for the firm of P.A. & S. Small before apprenticing to carpenter William Gotwalt in 1869 and going to work for Nathaniel Weigel, a local carpenter. It was during this period that Dempwolf made full-size details of St. Paul's Church, located at the corner of West King and South Beaver Streets. This project was designed by Philadelphia architect Stephen D. Button.

Shortly thereafter, Dempwolf left York for New York, working as a construction foreman during the day and taking architectural drawing and design classes in the evening. He graduated from Cooper Union Institute in 1873 and then headed to Boston, where he superintended construction of the Holy Cross Catholic Church. One year later he was back in York and received his first design commission, First St. John's Lutheran Church on West King Street.

In 1875 he received an offer from Stephen D. Button to join him in Philadelphia to design buildings for Philadelphia's Centennial Exhibition. It was in Philadelphia that Dempwolf planned to remain, though York businessman Samuel Small was able to convince him to return to York and open an architectural practice. Fortunately for York, J.A. Dempwolf returned in 1876 and opened what was to become the most successful architectural practice in York County history. From the time the practice opened until 1920, the firm designed over six hundred buildings.

Dempwolf married Sallie A. Greiman in 1879 and was elected to the American Institute of Architects in 1901, helping to organize the local chapter in subsequent years. Dempwolf spent much of his adult life as superintendent of the Christ Lutheran Church Sunday school. He was a trustee of the York Collegiate Institute, Children's Home and YWCA, and a director of many companies, including York Trust Company, York Hospital & Dispensary and York Hotel Corp. In addition, he served as secretary for both the York Safe & Lock Company and York Foundry &

Machine Company. Dempwolf served on the Board of Managers for the York Benevolent Association, as president of the Historical Society of York County and chairman of the Pennsylvania State Art Council. He was also a member of the Lafayette Club, Art Club of Philadelphia and National Art Club of New York.

John Augustus Dempwolf died on December 24, 1926.

Emerton Family Home

863 South George Street

The stunning Emerton Family Home has been a landmark along South George Street for almost one hundred years. Constructed in 1916 from a design by J.A. Dempwolf, the 18,000-square-foot mansion was built by the Emerton family. Twelve years later, the Hahn Home was established here as a retirement home for elderly women. The property also includes a 2,700-square-foot caretaker's house.

Architecturally, the mansion is Tudor Revival with heavy, rough-cut Pennsylvania quartzite, arched windows, gabled parapets, stone mullions and balustrades. The north façade incorporates decorative half-timbering. The mansion houses a ballroom, formal foyer, library and eighteen bedrooms.

BEAVER STREET

York Telephone and Telegraph Building

31 South Beaver Street

Built in 1929 at a cost of $375,000, the York Telephone and Telegraph Building is one of York's most notable Art Deco buildings and was designed by Frederick Dempwolf. The company installed dial phone service in York in 1919, one of the earliest dial systems in the United States, and its telephone lines served multiple purposes. For instance, national radio broadcasts were transmitted to local stations via the lines, and the York Water Co. controlled pumping motors through the same lines.

While the stepped parapets and low-relief ornamentation define the building as Art Deco, other features include the high-relief globe and door grills. The latter was created by Paul Manship, who is best known for his work on Prometheus at Rockefeller Center in New York City. Prior to being installed on the building, the door grills were exhibited at the Metropolitan Museum of Art in New York. The façade is of Indiana limestone.

Beth Israel Synagogue

129 South Beaver Street

The Beth Israel congregation was organized in 1877 and originally met in members' homes. In 1907, this building was constructed as York's first Jewish temple. At the time, this area of York was nicknamed Little Moscow because of the diverse ethnic population. Originally, the temple was built to seat three hundred people, and there is beautiful stained glass visible on the inside. Interestingly, while a Star of David is present within the stained glass, so is a Masonic symbol; Nathan Lehmeyer, who built the temple, was an active member of the York Freemasons. Rabbi Alexander Goode, who led the temple prior to World War II,

resigned to join the military. In 1943, he was a chaplain serving aboard the USS *Dorchester* when a Nazi submarine sank it. Rabbi Goode and the ship's other three chaplains gave their life jackets to others. As the ship went down, they stood with their arms linked. History remembers the Four Chaplains for their brave sacrifice.

The temple is very architecturally unique. The façade has a polychromatic appearance with rounded arches, giving it a Victorian Romanesque feel. The roofline, however, is dominated by copper onion domes, adding a touch of Exotic Revival. Designed by York architect Charles Keyworth, the building today is now home to a Christian congregation.

Saint Patrick's Roman Catholic Church

229 South Beaver Street

The striking St. Patrick's Church opened in 1898, though the congregation dates from 1750 and was originally attended by missionaries from Baltimore,

Conewago and Emmitsburg. In 1776 the congregation began worshipping at a house located on this very site. A new church was constructed in 1810, followed by a school and meeting hall built on the rear of the property in the late 1880s. Construction on the current structure began in 1895 and was completed at a cost of almost $40,000.

Architecturally, the building is Late Gothic Revival and is one of the most elaborate churches in York. A large rose window dominates the front façade, though towers and pinnacles give the building its distinctive appearance. Note the heavy rough-cut stone and ribbon of arched windows on the tower to the right, which add a bit of Richardsonian style to an otherwise Gothic building.

Masonic Hall

15–17 North Beaver Street

Constructed in 1863, this building was originally a Masonic hall. Frederick Stallman, owner of the adjacent White Hall Hotel (see National House on West Market Street), was an active Mason and builder of the hall. Architecturally, it is a great example of an urban Gothic Revival building defined by its lancet or pointed arches. Other features include pointed hood molds, arched corbel table, shaped parapet and center pinnacle. At one time several pinnacles were present on the roofline, though they were later

removed. In 1911, the Masons purchased the former York Post Office, relocated and eventually constructed Gethsemane Hall next door.

Gethsemane Hall

111 North Beaver Street

Built in 1912 by the local Freemasons, Gethsemane Hall has a very unique, castle-like appearance. It was constructed after the Masons purchased the former York Post Office located next door, and the building served as their meeting hall. The rough-cut granite and round arch are characteristic of the Richardson Romanesque style, though the addition of towers with battlements and crenellated roofline transform the building into the Neo-Norman style, reflective of the English castles of the Norman period.

Episcopal Church of St. John the Baptist

130 North Beaver Street

The Episcopal Church of St. John the Baptist was founded in 1755 by the "Society for the Propagation of the Gospel in Foreign Parts." The original church on this site was constructed in 1769, and portions of the original walls and altar still exist. The building was expanded three times in the nineteenth century. York's Liberty Bell, the bell that was rung to celebrate the signing of the Declaration of Independence, is present inside the current Gothic Revival church. This same bell presided over the Second Continental Congress when York was capital of colonial America in 1777 and 1778.

During the American Revolution, the church was used as an arsenal. Perhaps one of the more interesting sidebars during the Continental Congress's stay in York was the duel that was planned to take place here. Colonel James Wilkinson, who was a staff member of General Horatio Gates, head of the Board of War, challenged Gates to a duel to settle a disagreement. However, Gates refused to arm himself against his aide.

Later, after leaving York, Wilkinson again challenged Gates to a duel. Again, Gates refused to arm himself, but this time Wilkinson fired three shots. All three missed their target.

The first local school of classical learning—and forerunner to today's York College of Pennsylvania—was established here. The onsite cemetery is one of the oldest burying places in the city of York. The remains of Colonel Thomas Hartley, York's first congressman, and Major John Clark, an aide to General Washington during the American Revolution, are interred here.

PHILADELPHIA STREET

Hoover Wagon Company

15 East Philadelphia Street

Known to longtime Yorkers as the *York Dispatch* Newsroom building, this 1886 structure was originally built by the Hoover Wagon Company, which was operated by George W. Hoover and his three sons. The company manufactured buggies and pleasure carriages. The *York Dispatch* moved into this building in 1904. The company had been founded in 1876 and originally published a four-page daily newspaper at a cost of one cent per copy.

In the building industry of today, "prefabricated" is a common term, and refers to constructing certain parts of a building—the structural system, for example—in a factory, and then delivering it to the construction site. Before the 1870s, this process was rare. However, as new technologies allowed cast iron to be mass produced, it became possible to build structures to new heights. Much of this cast iron was prefabricated, resulting in improved construction speed. Not only was it used for the structure of a building, but also for an exterior finish. York's most outstanding example of cast-iron architecture is the Hoover Wagon Co. Listed on the National Register of Historic Places, this building is Italianate in style and exemplifies the Commercial Italianate subtype. Notable features of this subtype include window pilasters, elaborate cornice and center parapet.

William Goodridge House

123 East Philadelphia Street

William C. Goodridge is one of the most interesting, if not enigmatic, personalities of nineteenth-century York. Born a slave, Goodridge came

to York when he was six and apprenticed to a local reverend and tanner. When he turned sixteen, he was given his freedom and left to study the trade of a barber. He later returned to York and became a barber on Centre Square. Goodridge was an aggressive entrepreneur and soon expanded his business to include a candy store, toys, daily newspapers and more. In time he would acquire twenty properties, construct York's first five-story building and begin the Goodridge Reliance Line—thirteen rail cars that serviced the region.

But much of Goodridge's private life is shrouded in mystery. He was an important conductor on the Underground Railroad, helping scores of escaped slaves find their way to freedom. His properties were stations along the Underground Railroad, and his rail cars contained hidden compartments to convey the escapees to freedom. It is believed that he constructed the house on East Philadelphia Street in the late 1820s, and lived there until at least 1859. While he eventually fell on financial hard times, he persevered, and as late as 1865 was still running advertisements for his barbershop in the local newspaper. Shortly thereafter he left York to join family members in Michigan, where his sons became pioneering photographers.

This house is listed on the National Park Service's Network to Freedom, a national database of authentic Underground Railroad locations. A Pennsylvania Historic Marker stands in front of the house, attesting to William Goodridge's importance. Inside, a root cellar originally accessible only by a hidden door in the kitchen floor gives further credence to the house's role as a station on the Underground Railroad.

Mr. Goodridge, however, was not the only notable resident of this home. In 1897, York architect Reinhardt Dempwolf and his wife purchased the house. Extensive renovations were soon completed. The original Federal façade was altered to a Colonial Revival appearance, incorporating a Georgian doorway from another home being demolished. The main parlor is quite elegant and features fluted Corinthian columns and a classic entablature. There is also an abundance of molding throughout the house—crown molding, chair rails and ornate fireplaces.

Central Market House

34 West Philadelphia Street

York has been a town of multiple markets since its beginnings. As early as 1754 there were two farmers' markets operating in the city. Market sheds were constructed in Centre Square, and stood until they were demolished in 1886.

Soon thereafter, local businessmen began to see the need for a new market house in the downtown area.

The Central Market House was organized one year later, and J.A. Dempwolf was commissioned in 1888 to design a new facility less than a block away from where the market sheds once stood. His unique L-shaped design incorporates five towers with pyramidal roofs. The façades on West Philadelphia and North Beaver Streets are almost identical. The exterior of the brick Victorian Romanesque building is defined by arches—arched entryways and ribbons of arched windows on the main elevations and towers. While Romanesque Revival buildings typically have a monochromatic appearance, this building incorporates brownstone accent bands and dark green paint for wooden elements. George Yinger was hired to construct the market, which cost $30,550 and opened in December 1888. Central Market has operated continuously since that time and is a must-see for downtown visitors As many as twenty thousand people have passed through the market doors in a single week during the busiest times.

Old York Post Office

55 West Philadelphia Street

Constructed in 1895, this building served as a post office until 1912, when a new, larger facility was built on South George Street. An 1890 Act of Congress appropriated $80,000 for construction of this facility, which also housed the U.S. Department of Revenue on the second floor. The building was designed under the direction of the Office of the Supervising Architect of the U.S. Treasury. During the period that the building was designed, architects Willoughby Edbrooke and Jeremiah O'Rourke both held that position. Edbrooke designed the Georgia State Capitol building, while O'Rourke was best known for designing prominent churches in New York City. After the federal government vacated the building, the local Masonic lodge relocated from their facility a half block away and later constructed Gethsemane Hall next door to serve as a meeting hall.

Architecturally, this is actually one of the most striking buildings within the city of York. It is Victorian Romanesque—that is, Romanesque Revival with a Victorian twist. The Beaver Street façade is more expansive, and features two towers as well as a cross-gabled roof intersection with the building's hipped roof. Squat imbedded columns support the massive sandstone arched entryways. The smaller tower is topped with a copper domed roof, while the larger tower is topped with a slate hexagonal roof. Note the ornamentation on the main tower, including gargoyles—which originally functioned as rainspouts—and grotesques between the arched windows.

York Meeting House

135 West Philadelphia Street

The Quakers were among the first settlers of York County, and in 1766 constructed this meetinghouse, which was subsequently expanded in 1783. One of the oldest religious facilities in the area, the Religious Society of Friends has been meeting here regularly since it first opened. The eastern portion of the building was built by William Willis, who also constructed the original York County Court House as well as his own home, known today as the Willis House. The building, which was originally symmetrical, utilizes Flemish bond brickwork with bricks imported from England. The purpose of the 1783 addition was to add a meeting room for women, who conducted their business separately from the men. Job Scott, a well-known Quaker preacher, spoke here in 1790. John Elgar, who constructed the first iron steamboat in America, is buried at the cemetery on this site.

Stevens School

606 West Philadelphia Street

The Stevens School is a notable example of Victorian Romanesque architecture. The building operated as an elementary school from 1890 until 1960, and was built at a cost of $15,985. Of the former city schools still in existence, the Stevens School is the second oldest.

The building was designed by J.A. and Reinhardt Dempwolf. The interior layout employs the Latin cross plan, while the exterior uses a variety of materials, including brownstone, brick, terra cotta and native limestone. The rounded entry arch defines the Romanesque style, while the "heavy" feel of the stone emphasizes a Richardsonian influence. The roof is hipped, with parapet wall dormers defining the roofline. Note the three windows with centered fanlight, which adds Palladian motif.

Elsewhere in York City

M.B. Spahr House

43 West King Street

Michael B. Spahr was a prominent
York business leader in the late
nineteenth century. He formed his
company, M.B. Spahr & Sons, in
the 1850s. Originally a wholesaler
and retailer, it wasn't until he
began stocking boots and shoes to
supply other stores that his business
began to grow. Spahr was a charter
member of Farmers' National Bank,

a trustee of the York County Academy—forerunner of York College—and
president of the York County Historical Society. On the northeast corner of
Continental Square he constructed a unique Second Empire building with
curved walls. This building was later torn down to make room for the First
National Bank building that stands there today.

On West King Street he built two Queen Anne homes, one for himself
and one for his daughter. The building at 43 West King Street, designed by
J.A. Dempwolf, is a high-style example and more elaborate than the second
home at the corner of West King and South Beaver Streets. The interior
of 43 West King features different wood—butternut, oak, cherry—in each
room. The bricks used to construct the home were imported from England,
and the etched stained-glass windows are notable.

York City Hall

50 West King Street

Even though much of York's architecture is Victorian, the community frequently defines itself as a colonial town, perhaps because of the important role York played during the American Revolution. As such, it is appropriate that York City Hall, which was constructed for a cost of $225,000, is Colonial Revival in style. It was built in 1941  to celebrate York's 200th anniversary, and features a prominent Neoclassical portico with colossal Ionic columns and dentilled pediment.

Architects Robert Stair and Frederick Dempwolf, in one of Dempwolf's last design commissions, drew inspiration from varied sources. The rooftop cupola was meant to pay homage to the cupola that sat atop the original York County Court House, while the lobby was designed to replicate Philadelphia's Independence Hall. The building contains many features typical of the Colonial Revival style, including pedimented doorways, raised basement, water table, belt course, keystones and dentilled cornice. The building's slate roof was quarried in Delta, York County.

Frederick Dempwolf's uncle, Reinhardt, collaborated to design the York City Seal, which is still in use today.

Rex and Laurel Firehouse

49–51 South Duke Street

Organized in the late 1700s, the Laurel Fire Company is one of the oldest fire companies in the United States. Originally, each member of the fire company was responsible for furnishing his own bucket. In 1798, the company acquired its first engine, and in 1840 the company purchased its first steam engine. By 1878, the company was in need of more space and the Laurel Fire House was built to honor the Borough of York and to showcase the pride of the company. Eight years later, the Rex Hook & Ladder Company was organized, and the Laurel Fire House was expanded. A two-horse truck was purchased in 1887 for $1,077, and a three-horse

Hays Truck was acquired in 1892 for approximately $5,000.

The striking Italianate firehouse features rounded arches, hood molds, quoins and bracketed eaves. The tower is characteristic of the Italian villa but features pointed arch openings, giving it a somewhat Gothic feel. The garage doors are topped with prominent pediments and a three-story tower is topped by a belfry with wrought-iron railing. A cream and brown color scheme is present on the building and is typical of the Victorian era. While several other Victorian firehouses remain in York City, the Rex and Laurel Firehouse is certainly the most notable.

Westminster Presbyterian Church

320 North Queen Street

Thirty-eight members of First Presbyterian Church formed the Westminster Presbyterian Church in 1887. The cornerstone of this building was laid on June 30, 1887, with the church being dedicated on December 15 of that same year. It was expanded five years later. Cassandra Small, who chronicled the Confederate occupation of York

through letters to her cousin in Baltimore, was a Sunday school teacher here.

The church was designed by the Dempwolf firm. It exhibits a Richardson Romanesque influence, particularly with its heavy, rough-cut stone. The main entrance combines a rounded Romanesque arch with a slightly pointed lancet arch.

This photograph was taken prior to construction of Sovereign Bank Stadium, home of the York Revolution minor league baseball team. Many of the buildings west of the church were demolished to make way for the stadium.

Cookes House

Martin Luther King Park/South Penn Street

Constructed by Johannes Cookes in 1761, this building is one of the oldest surviving structures in the city of York. During the tenure of the Second Continental Congress in York, it is believed that this building served as the residence of Thomas Paine, secretary to the Congressional Committee on Foreign Affairs. It is also believed that many national documents were kept here, some of which remained until 1903, when they were rediscovered and burned in the home's fireplace to provide heating. During the American Revolution, this home was one of the larger "suburban" dwellings, and the pastures that surrounded the house provided ample grazing for the horses of congressional delegates. While Paine was in York, he published No. 5 of a series of patriotic essays known as "The Crisis."

Architecturally, the building is German Colonial in style, evidenced by the asymmetrical façade and central chimney, though there is also somewhat of a formal appearance, indicating a Georgian influence. Arched stone lintels and a date stone on the front façade are also present. The bluish gray limestone Cookes House was placed on the National Register of Historic Places in 1972 and restored in the 1980s.

Farquhar Park Bandstand

Farquhar Park

This beautiful structure was constructed in 1903 and has hosted countless band concerts, weddings and family reunions over the past century. Farquhar Park was created in 1897 when local industrialist Arthur Briggs Farquhar donated land to create a park. The York Board of Park Commissioners was soon established, thirty-two acres of additional land were acquired and Farquhar Park was dedicated in 1898. The bandstand, which was designed by John Hamme and Edward Leber, is notable for its tall Doric columns as well as its tricolored slate roof. Additional architectural features include brackets and dentils. By the late 1990s, the structure had fallen into a state of disrepair, and it was eventually closed to the public. A 2002 restoration returned the bandstand to its original glory.

Frick House

100 West Springettsbury Avenue

Constructed in 1910, this was the home of Charles C. Frick, a banker and musician. J.A. Dempwolf designed the 9,450-square-foot mansion, which was built for $16,732. Interior spaces originally included reception and concert halls. Frick was prominent in the local community and served as vice-president and director of the

Security Title and Trust Co. and director of Hoover Carriage Works. He was also an original director and treasurer of York Telephone Co. and treasurer of Norway Iron & Steel Co. His love of music led him to become treasurer of the York Oratorio Society.

Architecturally, the building is Colonial Revival with a Neoclassical portico exhibiting colossal Corinthian columns. The hipped roof is truncated and has a railing, a feature known as a captain's walk or widow's walk and a common design element for coastal architecture. Palladian windows are located to the sides of the portico on the first level, and a half-round window adds character to the pediment. Jeffersonian Classicism, referring to the designs of Thomas Jefferson and those who followed, frequently incorporated a half-round window within a classical portico.

Old York County Jail

319 Chestnut Street

York's first jail was established in 1750 at the northeast corner of South George and East King Streets. It was replaced in 1768 by a new structure on the same site. As York grew, the idea of having a jail so close to the town square was deemed inappropriate, and a new castle-like jail was built near the York County Almshouse on Chestnut Street in 1854. By the early twentieth century, a new jail was required to house the growing prison population.

Local architect B.F. Willis was commissioned to design this Italian Renaissance building, which was completed in 1906. The six-story brick and limestone building was used as a prison until 1979, at which time it was vacated. It has stood empty ever since. In 2003, the National Trust for Historic Preservation conducted a Leadership Training Conference in York. Participants were divided into five groups, each evaluating the former prison to develop a plan to rehabilitate the structure. Recommended solutions included a community arts center, vocational school and mixed-use space, among others.

Philip King House

427 Kings Mill Road

In 1798, Philip King opened a small paper mill southwest of downtown York. The site was chosen due to its location at the convergence of the beautiful Tyler Run and Codorus Creek. Mr. King made paper using minimal equipment, creating pulp from linen rags and making one sheet at a time. One of two watermarks— "P.J.K." or "KING"—was pressed onto the paper. By 1812, Philip and his wife, Catharine, had constructed a stately manor house.

The King House is a prominent example of Federal architecture, a favored style of architects within the young nation. The prominent entrance features an arched pediment with dentils, pilasters, rosettes and a transom light. The arched feature above the doorway exemplifies the Federal style, which also frequently incorporated a fanlight above the main entrance. The roof is gabled and includes three dormers with arched pediments. A water table is present, and brickwork is of the Flemish bond.

Willis House

Willis Run/Prospect Hill Cemetery

Constructed in 1762, the William Willis House is an important example of York's Georgian architecture. William Willis was a Friend (Quaker) and mason who helped to build the original York County Court House as well as the Friends Meeting House in York. His son, Samuel Willis, continued to live in the house after

his father's death, becoming an agent on the Underground Railroad and using this home and property as a station. The home has been recognized by the National Park Service Network to Freedom program, which designates authentic Underground Railroad sites throughout the nation.

The interior is based upon a variant of the center hall design. As was common with the Georgian style, the building exhibits a symmetrical front façade, end chimneys, water table and a steeply pitched gable roof. The brickwork is Flemish bond, and Willis was able to demonstrate his talent as a mason by making all the bricks used for construction. In the western gable he placed glazed headers with "W W 1762"—his initials and the year the house was constructed. The front façade has a pent roof, a common feature of local Georgian construction.

YMCA of York and York County

90 North Newberry Street

The YMCA came to York in 1855 and was formally organized in 1868 at First Presbyterian Church. Members met at fire companies, and eventually purchased a building at 140 West Market Street and constructed a gymnasium, hall and swimming pool. In 1922, members began a campaign to raise money for a new building. They exceeded their goal of $525,000 by over $65,000. Construction commenced, and the new building with 158 dorm rooms was dedicated in 1926.

The YMCA building incorporates the Colonial Revival style, though it also employs some Italian Renaissance features similar to those found on the Yorktowne Hotel, which opened a year earlier. Both buildings feature rustication, distinct horizontal divisions and smaller windows on the attic story. Additionally, the YMCA features a prominent broken pediment above the main entrance, keystones and a quoining effect at the corners. And while the Yorktowne Hotel uses massive two-story arched windows to draw visual emphasis above street level, the YMCA's main level is raised above street level and is accessible via an external staircase. This feature is known as piano nobile.

George Whiteley House

905 South Beaver Street

This striking Tudor Revival home was constructed at the intersection of South Beaver Street and Springettsbury Avenue. It was originally located adjacent to the nine-hole golf course of the Country Club of York, but today the York College of Pennsylvania is its neighbor. The house was completed in the early 1900s by George H. Whiteley, an executive with the Dentist's Supply Company. Whiteley was born in New Jersey in 1857, and spent much of his earlier career involved with different businesses throughout the United States. He ran a store in Minnesota, a stationary and printing company in Colorado and eventually became involved with dental manufacturing businesses in Philadelphia, Delaware and New York. In 1899, Whiteley went together with three friends and founded the Dentist's Supply Company. The offices were originally in New York and the

manufacturing plant was established in York. The company, today known as Dentsply, is headquartered in York and is the largest manufacturer of dental prosthetics and consumable dental products in the world.

The picturesque house is defined by decorative half-timbers and gables. Two prominent front-facing gables and two gabled dormers create a charming roofline, while an extremely large wraparound porch, with its own gable, adds to the storybook appearance. The house was designed by the firm of Hamme and Leber.

The Tudor Revival style was popular in the late nineteenth and early twentieth centuries, particularly for houses. The decorative half-timbers so prominent in the style date back to the Elizabethan era; however, only about half of Tudor Revival buildings actually have half-timbers.

Codorus Creek Bridge

Codorus Creek near Cottage Hill Road

In 1884, York experienced a devastating flood that wiped out all of the bridges throughout the town. In fact, a high-water mark on the nearby Variety Iron Works building is testament to the severity of the flooding. Afterward, the county commissioners funded replacement bridges at Market, King, Philadelphia, Princess, George and Penn Streets. These iron bridges had an erector set–type appearance, similar to the bridge pictured here. All of those bridges were replaced in subsequent years, most recently the North George Street bridge, which was replaced in 2001.

The bridge pictured here was constructed for the Western Maryland Railroad, which operated both a passenger terminal and freight terminal near the Codorus Creek along North George Street.

Soldiers and Sailors Monument

Penn Park

From the early days of York's existence, Penn Common has played an important role for the community. Named for the family who founded Pennsylvania, the public commons has served as a fairgrounds, public park and military facility. During the American Revolution, troops were mustered and camped here. Penn Common was the site of the execution of several Continental soldiers during the Revolution. General "Mad" Anthony Wayne, who was in York recruiting men for the Yorktown campaign, ordered four men to be executed for minor offenses, like drinking and cursing,

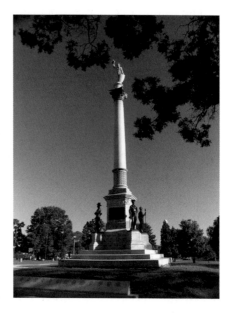

in order to maintain discipline. During the Civil War, a major U.S. Army hospital was constructed here. The hospital had several buildings and could hold over one thousand wounded at a time. Throughout the war, over fourteen thousand soldiers were treated here. Many of those who died are today buried in Prospect Hill Cemetery. During the Confederate occupation of York, soldiers from North Carolina seized the hospital and camped on the grounds.

In the late nineteenth century, Penn Common experienced major improvements and transitioned to Penn Park. A new bandstand was constructed, walking paths were created, large new fountains were built and tennis courts were installed. The Soldiers and Sailors monument was dedicated on June 15, 1898. It was designed by the Dempwolf architectural firm to honor those who gallantly fought in the Civil War. The monument is topped with the *Statue of Victory* and was funded by the county commissioners at a cost of $23,500.

Grace Reformed Church

225 North Hartley Street

While most Christian churches constructed during the Victorian era are either Romanesque Revival or Late Gothic Revival in style, Grace Reformed Church exhibits an eclectic late Victorian design. Construction on the church began in 1886, and the congregation occupied the building two years later. At first glance, the building is of the Shingle style popular during the period: shingle-clad façade, stone first level. However, this unique building incorporates lancet or pointed arches, a defining feature of Gothic architecture. Combining features from multiple styles was a hallmark of the late Victorian era, whether incorporating exotic influences from Egypt and Asia with a "traditional" design, or a more subtle approach, as is the case with Grace Reformed Church.

The church was organized by the pastor of Trinity Reformed Church, and opened with thirty-seven charter members. Due to rapid early growth of the church, a parsonage was constructed in the early 1890s, with a new two-story Sunday school building opening in 1898.

The Avenues

Northwest York, commonly called the Avenues, is a National Register of Historic Places historic district. The neighborhood had its beginnings in 1882, when William H. Lanius purchased fifty-two acres of land northwest of downtown York for $360 per acre. The "Captain," as Lanius was known, was a veteran of the Civil War and president of the York Trust Company. He established the West End Improvement Company in 1884 to develop the land to include both "town" and "cottage" lots. Lanius also formed the York Street Railway Company, which provided trolley service via Roosevelt and Linden Avenues, making the Avenues York's first streetcar suburb. By 1886, twenty-eight homes had been constructed, with most ranging in cost from $1,500 to $2,000.

The neighborhood showcases a variety of late Victorian and early twentieth-century architectural styles—Queen Anne, Colonial Revival, Prairie, Bungalow and even a few examples of Stick, Shingle and Second Empire. Larger "cottage" homes can be found on the hill around Farquhar Park, while the "town" homes are located between Roosevelt and Carlisle Avenues. Many of the homes—both single family and detached—feature Eastlake detailing.

Many prominent York residents called the Avenues home, including William Lanius, who resided at 401 Roosevelt Avenue. Another prominent resident was General Jacob Devers, a four-star general who accepted the surrender of German forces in Austria during World War II. George Whiteley, who co-founded the Dentist's Supply Company, also owned a home here. Other prominent residents included Walter Young, publisher of the *York Dispatch*; Karl Katz, owner of Katz Brewing Company; and Thomas Shipley, general manager of the York Manufacturing Company, which became York International Corp. and is today part of Johnson Controls. J. Horace Rudy, owner of the nationally prominent Rudy Bros. Leaded & Stained Glass Co., also resided in the Avenues.

Locust Street

300 Block

The Locust Street neighborhood is a hidden gem located off the beaten path. In the mid-1800s, the land was part of the York Fairgrounds, serving as Camp Scott during the Civil War. After the fairgrounds relocated to the western part of York City, the land became attractive for development. While there are a few Queen Anne single-family homes,  most of the street comprises attractive townhouses constructed in the first decade of the twentieth century. As the suburbs grew in prominence, the beautiful homes on this block fell into a state of disrepair. Fortunately, a major redevelopment initiative in the late 1980s returned many of these buildings to their original splendor. Locust Street is really an urban oasis unto itself. The beautiful townhouses are defined by colorful oriels and railings. The neighborhood is York's version of Philadelphia's Elfreth's Alley, though the Locust Street homes are all Victorian, not Colonial. At the intersection of Locust Street and South Pine Streets sits a large Queen Anne home that was constructed in 1895 and was once the home of Jacob Beitzel, who served as president and a director of Drovers and Mechanics Bank.

The York County Agricultural Society was formed in 1853 and two years later purchased 7.5 acres in the southeastern section of town to construct exhibition space for annual events. At the time, the fair lasted for just three days. The fairgrounds eventually expanded to 14 acres, and receipts from the fairs were used to construct and maintain buildings. The fair continued to grow in popularity, and in 1887 the York County Agricultural Society purchased land to construct a new fairgrounds on the western edge of the city.

South Newberry Street

The South Newberry Street/Newton Square area is a great example of urban neighborhood redevelopment. Comprising mostly Federal and Greek Revival townhouses constructed in the mid-nineteenth century, the neighborhood lay in ruin in 1972 after Tropical Storm Agnes dumped

several inches of rain on York, sending the Codorus Creek over its banks and causing millions of dollars in damage. Most of the homes on South Newberry Street were no longer fit to live in. Some in the community wanted the neighborhood raised and replaced with warehouses and light manufacturing facilities, expanding the city's tax base. However, a group of concerned community leaders saw the potential of the neighborhood and a "Back to the City" program was launched to encourage reinvestment in the now blighted community. A combination of marketing and low-interest loans lured home buyers to the neighborhood, eventually resulting in over sixty historic homes being rehabilitated. Often compared to Fell's Point or Federal Hill in Baltimore, or even Alexandria, Virginia, the South Newberry Street neighborhood offers similar housing for just a fraction of the cost of those areas. Today, a stroll on the first two blocks of South Newberry Street reveals many treasurers—tree-lined brick sidewalks, wrought-iron railings and details, attractive brick homes, prominent Greek Revival entrances and even a horse hitching post.

Springdale Neighborhood

In 1894, Grier Hersh constructed a golf course on his estate, Springdale, introducing many Yorkers to the game. Another prominent citizen, A.B. Farquhar, became so enamored with the sport that he went together with Hersh to establish the Country Club of York and construct a new nine-hole golf course west of South George Street. Hersh then decided to subdivide part of his estate into tracts for attractive housing. Ever since, Springdale has been the grandest of York's historic neighborhoods. The neighborhood instantly attracted many of York's wealthy, who liked the suburban feel and the easy access to the downtown via streetcar lines on South George Street and South Queen Street, which bordered the neighborhood.

Springdale has an eclectic collection of architecture with many early twentieth-century styles: Colonial Revival, Tudor Revival, Spanish Colonial Revival, French Eclectic and Bungalow. Interestingly, many of the grand homes were actually constructed during the Great Depression, a testament to York's prominent past regardless of the national economy. Throughout the past century, many of York's leading citizens have called Springdale home.

The Springdale property was originally constructed in the 1820s by Charles Barnitz, a prominent local citizen and U.S. Congressman. So

well-known was Barnitz that he served as legal counsel to William Penn's heirs and his home is believed to have been designed by Benjamin Latrobe, architect of the U.S. Capitol. Barnitz's grandson, Grier Hersh, eventually owned the estate, which he expanded to forty rooms. Hersh was prominent in his own right, serving as president of the York Bank and York County Gas Company. The original mansion was demolished in 1954, though a Victorian Eclectic–style carriage house from the property still stands along North Duke Street. In 2001, the neighborhood became a historic district listed on the National Register of Historic Places, with 199 contributing buildings.

Fairmount Historic District

North Beaver Street

With 101 contributing buildings, the Fairmount Historic District is the smallest National Register of Historic Places historic district within the city of York. The Victorian neighborhood is located along North Beaver Street and was laid out in 1884 by Edward W. Spangler, a developer, journalist, attorney and business owner. His goal was to create a middle- and upper-class neighborhood with homes set back from the sidewalks, creating yards and open spaces.

The neighborhood is an example of Victorian Eclecticism, with many homes incorporating features of the Queen Anne, Second Empire, Gothic Revival, Colonial Revival and Italianate styles. Some buildings were primarily designed in one style; others incorporate several. There is also a fine example of the Shingle style in the neighborhood. All contributing buildings in the district are residential. Along North Beaver Street the homes are detached and semidetached, while the side streets contain row houses.

YORK COUNTY

Accomac Inn

Accomac Road near Wrightsville

Today regarded as one of the finest restaurants in central Pennsylvania, the Accomac Inn has a long and storied history. The land on which the inn sits was the first tract of land granted on the west bank of the Susquehanna River. Sometime in the 1730s, James Anderson began operating a ferry between Marietta, Lancaster County, and the area known as Accomac. In 1742 Anderson's Ferry was granted an official charter from the Province of Pennsylvania. Anderson's Ferry Inn was constructed prior to 1775 and is believed to have played host to delegates of the Second Continental Congress en route to York Town to govern the young nation in 1777–78. French nobleman Marquis de Lafayette penned two letters from Anderson's Ferry in early 1778, and General Horatio Gates is believed to have taken Anderson's Ferry en route to York Town to serve in his new duty as president of the Board of War.

In the late 1800s, the area became known as Accomac, which is believed to be an alternative spelling of Acaumauke, a Nanticoke word meaning "on the other side." The original building caught fire in 1935, and much of it was destroyed. However, the inn was immediately rebuilt using the foundation, stones and floor plan of the earlier structure.

Codorus Furnace

Codorus Furnace Road at Codorus Creek

The Codorus Furnace was constructed in the mid-1830s on the site of a forge that had been operating since the 1760s. James Smith, a signer of the Declaration of Independence who is buried at First Presbyterian Church

in York City, once owned the forge. During the American Revolution, the forge produced cannons and cannonballs for the Continental army. The thirty-foot-tall Codorus Furnace is notable for its age, condition and design—round furnaces were uncommon during the era in which it was constructed. This structure is listed on the National Register of Historic Places (Codorus Forge and Furnace Historic District), along with the nearby ironmaster's house and remnants of the original forge.

Columbia-Wrightsville Bridge

Susquehanna River at Wrightsville

The famed Lincoln Highway bisects York County, passing through the city of York and eventually into Lancaster County via the Columbia-Wrightsville Bridge. This incarnation of the bridge was dedicated on Armistice Day in 1930, and was the longest multiple-arch concrete bridge in the world when constructed. The bridge, which has forty-eight spans and twenty-eight arches, is approximately 1¼ miles long. Four prior bridges crossed the Susquehanna River at this site, including three covered bridges (among the longest covered bridges in the world) and one metal truss bridge. The first

covered bridge was constructed in 1814 and was destroyed by an ice jam in 1832. The second bridge was destroyed in 1863 by Union troops fleeing the Confederate army. The Confederates had hoped to capture the bridge, allowing access to Lancaster, Philadelphia or Harrisburg from the undefended eastern side. By 1868 a new covered bridge had been constructed, and this one lasted until it was destroyed during an 1896 windstorm. The piers from the earlier bridges still stand today, adjacent to the current bridge. Note the Art Deco features of the Columbia-Wrightsville Bridge.

Wallace-Cross Gristmill

Cross Mill Road, Crossroads

Placed on the National Register of Historic Places in 1977, the historic Wallace-Cross Gristmill along Rambo Creek has been restored by the York County Parks Department. The mill was standing 1840, and may have been constructed as early as 1826 by Alexander Wallace. It operated continuously until Harry Cross donated it to the county in 1979. This country mill, which relied upon water power and a millstone grinding process for a century and a half, stands as a rare example of the rural mill common throughout Pennsylvania in the nineteenth century. Timbers were hand hewn and beams were assembled using a "tongue and pin" process. Originally, the mill used two stones to grind grain for the family and their animals. When built, the mill featured a wood overshot wheel with wooden spokes and shaft. Today, a Fitz water wheel, which was manufactured in Hanover in the 1920s, can be seen during the various public open houses held throughout the year. The mill's restoration reflects its appearance in the 1950s.

Hanover Junction Rail Station

Route 616, Hanover Junction

Restored to its 1863 appearance by the York County Department of Parks and Recreation, this picturesque train station has an impressive history. Constructed in 1852 along the National Central Railroad, Hanover Junction played an important role during the Civil War. The Northern Central Railroad was used to transport Union soldiers and supplies from the north and west to Baltimore and points south, making it a target during the Confederate invasion of Pennsylvania. In late June 1863, White's Commanches—under the leadership of Colonel Elijah White—rode through southern York County, cutting the telegraph lines at Hanover Junction and destroying nearby bridges. Even Union General George Meade had his eyes on Hanover Junction: "I shall push on tomorrow in the direction of Hanover Junction and Hanover, when I hope by July 2 to open communication with Baltimore by telegraph and rail, to renew supplies." Meade telegraphed this message on the eve of the Battle of Gettysburg and subsequently changed course to engage the Confederate army concentrating west of York County.

During the battle, the telegraph station at Hanover Junction was critical for relaying messages between Union battlefield commanders and their superiors in Washington, D.C. By mid-July, the destroyed bridges had been rebuilt and the rail lines reopened, allowing equipment and supplies to be sent and the wounded to be evacuated from Gettysburg. In total, over 11,000 wounded—including 7,600 Federal and 3,800 Confederate troops—were processed through the station in the weeks following the Battle of Gettysburg. Members of the Christian Commission fed and tended to the wounded soldiers, who were then sent north to hospitals in York and Harrisburg or south to hospitals in Baltimore. Some wounded were sent as far away as New York. On November 18, 1863, President Abraham Lincoln switched trains at the station en route to the dedication of the National

Cemetery, where he gave the Gettysburg Address. He switched trains again the following day on his return trip to Washington, D.C. Lincoln's funeral train also passed through Hanover Junction on April 21, 1865. Today, the restored structure contains a small Civil War museum and is listed on the National Register of Historic Places.

Indian Steps Museum

Indian Steps Road, Airville

Constructed in 1912 by York attorney John Edward Vandersloot, the Indian Steps Cabin—as it was originally known—is probably one of the most unique Craftsman homes in the United States. Several thousand Native American artifacts of stone and ceramic collected by the owner are embedded in the façade. The foundation and first story were primarily constructed of local fieldstone; however, cement panels were also incorporated for various inscriptions and embedding of artifacts. The second story is stucco, and a dominant fieldstone tower is located on the rear corner. The main building and tower feature pyramidal roofs, while the projecting central pavilion features a gabled roof. Roof eaves are wide and feature extended

timbers, a common element of the Craftsman style. Other prominent Craftsman features present are battened doors and wrought-iron hinges. The Susquehannock Indians were the first residents of York County, long before any European stepped foot in North America, and the Indian Steps Museum is one of the oldest museums in the country specifically dedicated to Native American culture and artifacts. Indian Steps Museum is operated by the Conservation Society of York County.

Haines Shoe House

Shoe House Road, Hellam

Mahlon Haines, known both as the "Shoe Wizard" as well as an eccentric philanthropist, constructed the Shoe House in 1947 as a way to promote his business. The building was actually livable, and he was known to lend it free of charge to newlyweds, who were serviced by the live-in butler and maid. Haines also opened the odd home to elderly couples. Legend has it that he hired an architect, handed him a shoe and said, "Build this." The end result was a stucco boot standing twenty-five feet in height and forty-eight feet in length. In addition to the various bedrooms and living spaces, the Shoe House also featured a rooftop, or "shoetop," observation platform. This unique structure was built along the Lincoln Highway, and is today nationally recognized as one of the best surviving examples of roadside architecture.

Johannes and Cristina Schultz House

508 Locust Grove Road, Springettsbury Township

The Johannes and Cristina Schultz House is one of the oldest surviving houses in York County. Several members of the Schultz family came from Friedelsheim in the Palatinate region of Germany in 1732. Until recently, it was believed that Johannes and Cristina Schultz were with the family; however, recent research has revealed that they apparently didn't arrive in the country until 1742. Johannes eventually constructed his home along the Monocacy Road and operated a two-hundred-acre plantation. In 1783, the plantation became Camp Security, home to British and Canadian prisoners captured during the American Revolution. The British soldiers were captured at Saratoga, New York, while the Canadians were caught in

Yorktown, Virginia. A stockade and village were constructed on the Schultz plantation and later removed.

This house has an interesting mystery that has yet to be solved. The date stone of the German Colonial home translates as, "In the year 1734 Johannes Schultz and Cristina my wife have built this house." However, if they didn't actually arrive until eight years later, why does the date stone read 1734? The substantial house is fairly unique in that it was constructed of stone, unlike most of the homes of that period, which were built of logs. It is two and a half stories in height and four bays in width. A pent roof on the front façade was present at one time. The interior floor plan is large enough to allow a central hall and two end chimneys, though the house originally featured a central chimney. The home also has a vaulted cellar.

Martin Schultz House

Emig Street, Hallam

Dating from 1736, the Martin Schultz House is one of the oldest homes in York County. Like his brother Johannes, Martin Schultz had a large expanse of land, including the mill known today as Macklay's Mill on South Broad

Street. Thomas Penn granted 226 acres of land to Hans Martin Schultz. Martin was also a founder of Kreutz Creek Lutheran Church.

The blue limestone home is built into a bank and is one and a half stories at the front elevation and three bays wide. The steeply pitched roof originally featured a central dormer with shed roof. The current roof dormers and porch were added in 1956, though the home otherwise retains much of its historical character. It is German Colonial in style with central chimneys and vaulted cellar.

"Hermit House"

East York

Located in East York near Pleasant Acres, the so-called Hermit House, or Fisher House, is believed to have been constructed around 1785, though some sources indicate a construction date as early as the 1740s. The home was once the Chestnut Hill Iron Ore Weighing Station. Curvin Houser, a hermit, lived here for many years. He farmed the nearby fields but had no heat, electricity, plumbing or running water, even though he lived here in the mid-twentieth century.

Like the Martin Schultz House, the building is built into a bank and is one and a half stories at the front elevation and three bays wide. Unlike the Schultz house, however, the chimneys are located at the ends, perhaps indicating the growing influence of Georgian architecture on German Colonial buildings. The house also features quoins and dormers with shed roofs. Today a private residence, the building was restored in the late 1960s.

"Hobbit House"

55 South Yale Street, Elmwood

The "Hobbit House," as this building is sometimes referred, is fairly unique for York County. It was designed by Russell Yessler, son of architect Harry Yessler. The elder Yessler actually helped design the Elmwood neighborhood and many of the houses in it. The house was originally the residence of Harry J. McDevitt of Martin-Parry Corp.

Architecturally, the building is of the Tudor Revival style. The distinctive false-thatched roof is a subtype of the style, and emulates the storybook Cotswold cottages of rural England.

Boxhill Manor

Spring Garden

George and Purdon (Smith) Whiteley purchased a large expanse of land south of York City in 1926 and commissioned Frederick Dempwolf, a family friend, to design their home. George Whiteley was president of Dentsply, a company co-founded by his father. At one point the estate, named for Box Hill in England, encompassed five hundred acres. Mrs. Whiteley had watched her parents' home (Brockie Mansion) burn years earlier, and wanted the new home to be as fireproof as possible.

Formal gardens were constructed first, followed by the stately Colonial Revival home. The formal façade has many notable features, including a prominent Palladian window above the entrance, which itself features a broken swan's neck pediment with pineapple finial. Stone quoins and keystones accent the brick façade. The roof is hipped and features

prominent dormers and chimneys. The small round window above the Palladian window is sometimes referred to as a bull's-eye window. While Frederick Dempwolf is credited with the design, his uncle Reinhardt was also probably heavily involved with the project.

Brockie Mansion

Spring Garden

The visually stunning Brockie Mansion is actually the second home on this site to bear that name. Jeremiah Sullivan Black, former U.S. attorney general and secretary of state, constructed the first Brockie Mansion in 1873. His beautiful Second Empire home hosted many famous Americans, including President James Garfield and Union General Winfield Scott Hancock. Black died in 1883 and his son, Pennsylvania Lieutenant Governor Chauncey F. Black, moved in. In 1906 C. Elmer Smith, president of S. Morgan Smith and Company, purchased the mansion, which was destroyed by fire several years later. The second Brockie Mansion was constructed in 1912, though the carriage house and other features from the original mansion remain.

Like many other local mansions constructed in the early twentieth century, Brockie combines a Colonial Revival design with a Neoclassical portico. The colossal columns are topped by Scamozzi capitals, which are also sometimes referred to as Greek Angular Ionic or Modern Ionic. The capitals are named for sixteenth-century Italian architect Vincenzo Scamozzi, who changed the Greek Ionic order to have four volutes angled at forty-five degrees. Thomas Jefferson employed this type of capital in the design of the Virginia State House.

Dritt Mansion

Long Level

The Dritt Mansion was constructed around 1758 by George Stevenson, an agent of the Penn family and keeper of records when York County was formed. The most famous resident of the home was General Jacob Dritt, who commanded a company of Pennsylvania militia during the American Revolution. He was captured by the British at Fort Washington and taken prisoner. After the war, Dritt established a plantation along the Susquehanna River. Dritt owned a liquor store on Centre Square in York and maintained

a business transporting goods—particularly wine and liquor—along the Susquehanna River. He returned to the Pennsylvania militia in 1800 as a brigadier general. In 1817, Dritt visited family members on the Columbia side of the river. While returning home, his boat collided with ice and he subsequently drowned.

The home is believed to have been built on the foundation of Cresap's Fort, which was built by Thomas Cresap in the 1730s. At the time, Lord Baltimore of Maryland claimed the land and Cresap moved here and recruited German families to locate on 150 acres of land that he called Pleasant Gardens. Cresap convinced the families that they were purchasing land in Maryland. Pennsylvania issued a warrant for his arrest in 1736 and Cresap was captured and taken to Lancaster, then Philadelphia. He was later released and settled in western Maryland, where he is remembered as a pioneer and patriot. Of course, to the local residents he was better known as the "Maryland Monster" and the "Beast of Baltimore" because of the sometimes violent tactics he employed.

The mansion is constructed of fieldstone and exhibits Georgian features even though Pennsylvania German craftsmen constructed it. These features include end chimneys and symmetrical façade. The wraparound pent roof is also sometimes called a visor roof. Today, the mansion is known as the John & Kathryn Zimmerman Center for Heritage at Historic Pleasant Garden.

Elmwood Mansion

Elmwood

Elmwood Mansion has been an East York fixture since it was constructed in 1835 by Jacob Brillinger, a director of the York Bank and later a soldier for the Union army. At one time the property included a gristmill, distillery and creamery. John H. Small, a partner in the Billmeyer & Small Co. and manager of a lumber mill in Wrightsville, purchased the building and grounds in 1880. The house remained in the Small family until the 1950s. The building was originally located several hundred feet south of its current location. However, after one of the outbuildings caught fire, the Small family decided to relocate the magnificent home. Fred Small, son of John, had a vision to create a new planned community with wide boulevards. The neighborhood of Elmwood was born, and the mansion was relocated to anchor one end of Elmwood Boulevard. The name Elmwood comes from the large elm trees located on the property. The building remained a private residence until Memorial Hospital purchased it in 1985.

The mansion exhibits an antebellum plantation feel. It is Greek Revival in style, though the rounded porches and columns add a touch of Classical Revival.

Lower Grantley

Spring Garden

In the 1870s, George Small constructed a summer home south of York City and named it Grantley. Small was a son of prominent York businessman Philip Albright Small and led his father's business for many years. George Small and his wife primarily resided in Mount Vernon Place in Baltimore, where they entertained many distinguished individuals, including President Ulysses S. Grant. The name Grantley actually comes from Mrs. Small, whose maiden name was Grant. W. Latimer Small, a brother of George, also spent many summers at the Grantley mansion, which at the time included 120 acres of grounds.

In 1905, Latimer's son—also named George Small—constructed Lower Grantley on the family grounds. While the original Grantley is no longer in existence, Lower Grantley is still a private residence and exhibits a heavy

Neoclassical influence. Two colossal porticos remain; a third portico (seen on the left side of the photograph) was enclosed. A Palladian window dominates the pediment over the main entrance, and monumental columns are topped with Corinthian capitals. Splayed lintels, quoins and dentils all add to the formal look of the mansion.

Eltham

555 Highland Terrace, Spring Garden

Constructed in 1912 by S. Fahs Smith, Eltham is another of the impressive mansions constructed by York's business leaders on the hills south of York City. Smith was president of S. Morgan Smith and Company, which manufactured hydroelectric turbines for such places as Hoover Dam and Niagara Falls. George Motter, owner of George F. Motter & Sons, a manufacturer of printing presses, was the second owner of the estate. The Motter & Sons complex in York City is today home to the Agricultural & Industrial Museum operated by the York County Heritage Trust.

The Colonial Revival mansion features a Neoclassical portico with Doric capitals and a Palladian window. The roof and dormers are gabled. While many of the larger homes constructed during this period were brick, Eltham

employs rough-cut stone. A sizeable carriage house was subdivided from the main property and converted into a residence. Robert A. Stair was the architect of Eltham.

Ye Olde Valley Inn

Chestnut Hill Road, York Township

In 1738 John Greist, an English Quaker and one of the first settlers west of the Susquehanna River, constructed a two-story limestone home on the main east-west road through what was to become York County. Subsequent owners expanded the home and operated it as an inn and tavern. During 1777–78, when York served as the capital of colonial America, the tavern was frequented by members of the Continental Congress. For many years it was known as Hiestand Tavern, named for owner Abraham Hiestand. The building served as a station on the Underground Railroad and, in 1863, it is even believed that Confederate General John B. Gordon stopped here for refreshment before marching on Wrightsville. In 1962, the building was dismantled and relocated to Susquehanna Memorial Gardens near Dallastown, where it was rebuilt to its original dimensions.

The building is Georgian in design and features a balanced façade and two chimneys. Like many local Georgian structures from the eighteenth century, a pent roof—or visor roof, since it wraps around—is a prominent feature.

Warrington Meeting House

Wellsville

The Warrington Preparative Meeting was organized on September 2, 1747, and the congregation constructed this fieldstone structure in 1769 to replace a log meetinghouse dating from the 1740s. The structure features the typical simplicity of a Quaker meetinghouse with small, deeply set windows with protective shutters. The two front chimneys are original. In 1782 the meetinghouse was enlarged, doubling its size. The interior has been remarkably well preserved and exhibits the original hand-hewn beams and even hand-wrought nails. The Warrington Meeting House is one of two prominent Quaker meetinghouses in York County, the other being the York Meeting House on Philadelphia Street in York City.

The Nook

1101 Farquhar Drive, Spring Garden

Francis Farquhar constructed "The Nook" in 1893 on the grounds of his father's estate, Edgecombe. A.B. Farquhar, a prominent businessman for almost half a century, constructed his mansion in 1875. The Pennsylvania Agricultural Works, also known as A.B. Farquhar Company, was recognized internationally for its engines, boilers, sawmills, threshing machinery and more.

Francis Farquhar was a director of both the York National Bank and Guardian Trust Company, and helped organize the Manufacturers Association of York County in 1906.

The Nook is a striking Queen Anne building with shingle, clapboard and stucco elements on the façade. A prominent front-facing gable features decorative half-timbers, while a corner tower is topped with a polygonal roof.

Muddy Creek Forks

East Hopewell Township

This small village is located at the intersection of the Maryland and Pennsylvania Railroad and the Muddy Creek. It is fairly unique in that it was a self-contained village, connecting the area's agricultural base with the rest of the region via the railroad. The General Store/Station was constructed around 1900 by Alexander Grove. The main floor has two

entrances, one in the front for the general store and post office, and one on the side—facing the railroad tracks—for the station. When serving as a general store, the second floor of the building housed groceries, while the third floor contained clothing.

As early as the 1740s, a flour mill was operating on this site. The current gristmill, located across the street, was constructed in the mid-nineteenth century and expanded around 1890. The mill complex comprises three interconnected buildings: the mill; grain elevator and scalehouse; and fertilizer warehouse.

Rail came to Muddy Creek Forks in 1874 as the Peach Bottom Railway, which connected York and Delta. In 1901, the railroad became part of the Maryland and Pennsylvania Railroad. Passenger service ran until 1954, while freight service continued until 1978. Today, the village of Muddy Creek Forks is owned by the Maryland and Pennsylvania Preservation Society, which has restored much of the village and offers tours on select days.

Howard Tunnel

Northern Central Railway

The Howard Tunnel is one of the oldest continually operating rail tunnels in the world. It was completed in 1840, cut through three hundred feet of solid rock. During the Civil War, Pennsylvania militia guarded the tunnel to keep raiding Confederate cavaliers from sabotaging it. The Northern Central Railway was the main route for transporting soldiers and supplies from the north and west to Baltimore and beyond. In 1868, a second set of tracks was added and the tunnel entrances were renovated. The tunnel had originally been constructed wide enough to allow for two tracks. The entrances are of rough-faced ashlar stone and feature rustication and limestone date stones with the years 1840 (south entrance) and 1868 (north entrance). Today part of the York County Heritage Rail Trail County Park, the Howard Tunnel is not accessible by car. However, it is well worth the walk or bike ride to witness an important part of railroad history.

Wrightsville House

127–129 North Front Street, Wrightsville

Constructed around 1808, the Wrightsville House was once owned by John Kau Helt, a former sheriff of York County. For many years it served as a hotel. On June 28, 1863, after Pennsylvania militia had set fire to the Columbia-Wrightsville Bridge to halt the Confederate advance, sparks ignited the roof of this building. Wrightsville townspeople and Georgian soldiers stood side by side on bucket brigades to save structures and prevent the town from burning. The house is located in the Wrightsville Historic District, a National Register of Historic Places district with 350 contributing buildings.

Elmwood Neighborhood

Spring Garden Township

In the 1830s, Jacob Brillinger acquired land east of York City and constructed a gristmill, creamery and distillery, as well as a mansion that was completed in 1835.

Almost fifty years later, John Small of the Billmeyer and Small Co. purchased the property, though he and his family primarily lived in downtown York. He died in 1902 and his son Fred conceived of an idea to develop the Elmwood estate into a neighborhood. He commissioned architect Harry Yessler to develop a layout for the new neighborhood. The large mansion was relocated to the new Elmwood Boulevard. Streets were named after collegiate institutions attended by family members: Yale, Belmont, Wheaton and Ogontz.

The neighborhood contains a mix of architectural styles popular in the early twentieth century including Colonial Revival, Tudor Revival and Spanish Colonial Revival. Most of the homes were constructed in the 1920s and 1930s. The father-and-son architectural team of Harry and Russell Yessler designed many of the homes and Harry was actually a resident of the neighborhood.

Other prominent residents of the neighborhood have included Charles Zinn, president of Keystone Block Works; Harry Weinstock, owner of Acme Hosiery Co.; and Percy Mundorf, secretary of Weaver Piano Co.

Centre Presbyterian Church

New Park

York County's finest example of Richardson Romanesque architecture is Centre Presbyterian Church in New Park, not far from the Mason-Dixon line. The congregation dates from the 1700s, and it is believed that the name "Centre" is a reference to the location of the church, which is partway between previously established congregations at Round Hill and Bethel Presbyterian Churches. This building was constructed in 1888 from a design by York architect J.A. Dempwolf. The cost to construct it was $14,881, and an education building was eventually added in 1957.

The Richardson Romanesque style is named for Henry Hobson Richardson, who was the second American architect to study at the Parisian École des Beaux-Arts. He was a leading proponent of the Shingle style, but made a name for himself by combining Romanesque features into simple, massive stone buildings. Heavy, rough-cut stone and large, rounded arches define the style.

Guinston Presbyterian Church

Chanceford Township

Located near Airville, Guinston Presbyterian Church is one of the oldest surviving houses of worship in York County. The congregation was founded by Scots-Irish settlers in 1754; they built a log church that same year. The second church, which still stands, was constructed of local fieldstone in 1773. The building functioned as a church until 1867, at which time a new brick church was constructed and the old stone church became a Sabbath school. The brick church was destroyed by fire in 1946.

A 1972 project preserved much of the 1773 building. It is thirty feet wide and forty-six feet long, with entrances in the gabled ends. Window and door openings feature stone arches, while the roof and eaves are of slate.

Red Lion Historic District

There are over 1,480 contributing buildings in the Red Lion Historic District. The town was founded as a railroad stop in 1874, situated on the gentle rolling hills of central York County. The Maryland and Pennsylvania

Railroad allowed the town to grow and prosper, while two wagon roads provided access to other local communities. Red Lion was in some ways a melting pot, with German, Swiss, Scots-Irish and English constituting the early residents. The name "Red Lion" comes from the mid-nineteenth-century Red Lion Tavern, which no longer stands.

The majority of buildings in the borough are residential, and duplexes are common. The largest structures are industrial in nature, many dating from the period when Red Lion was known as a major production location for both furniture and tobacco, the latter of which included tobacco preparation, cigar making and cigar box manufacturing. Several Late Gothic Revival churches, like Bethany United Brethren, can be found within the historic district. There are also a few examples of Renaissance Revival style, like the Hill School. Residential styles are varied, but are for the most part Victorian and early twentieth century. A few high-style Queen Anne houses stand out among the Colonial Revival, Craftsman and American Foursquare homes that are far more common. Several of the larger buildings have been adaptively reused into apartments. These include the 1921 Consumers Cigar Box Company and 1914 Red Lion Opera House.

Shrewsbury Historic District

Strasburg was settled in the eighteenth century and was later renamed Shrewsbury. It is one of the oldest towns in York County and was incorporated as a borough in 1834. The Baltimore-York Turnpike, established in 1810, has been a major factor for the town's growth. The road was actually a path to freedom along the Underground Railroad for slaves escaping from Maryland. When the railroad was established in 1838, passing within a mile of Shrewsbury, the town enjoyed further prosperity.

Several log houses from the eighteenth century still remain in the historic district. In total, there are over twenty-five log houses. As a center of southern York County agriculture, Shrewsbury's greatest period of growth

was between 1800 and 1850, as the town transitioned from a residential community to a center of commerce. The Shrewsbury Historic District was placed on the National Register of Historic Places in 1984 and today Main Street offers a charming stroll through yesteryear as it maintains much of its mid-nineteenth-century look.

Spring Grove Historic District

In 1747, Spring Forge was laid out on the west branch of the Codorus Creek, not far from the Pigeon Hills. Originally home to the first iron forge west of the Susquehanna River (circa 1770), the town found its identity in 1852 when the iron buildings were converted for paper manufacturing. In 1863, P.H. Glatfelter and Martin Laucks purchased the mill for $14,000 and the renamed Spring Grove became a "company town." With the paper mill's success came a rapid growth of the town, which was enhanced by the addition of rail service in 1876 as well as a trolley line, which ran from 1908 to 1939.

The paper mill constructed housing, which it sold to the workers. The National Register of Historic Places historic district was established in 1984 and has 175 contributing buildings. Notable buildings include the 1887 Aldine Hotel, 1897 Spring Grove Public School and 1912 Glatfelter Mansion.

East York Historic District

The East York Historic District, which is listed on the National Register of Historic Places, was established in the late 1990s. The neighborhood was laid out in 1903 to the east of Elmwood and, until the construction of Interstate-83, the two neighborhoods were actually connected. East York is primarily residential, with a handful of commercial buildings along East Market Street.

The buildings showcase a variety of early twentieth-century styles, including Colonial Revival, Tudor Revival, Craftsman and French Eclectic. The larger buildings include a 1936 Art Deco apartment building and Second Empire house. Trolley service was established in 1903, connecting East York with the city to the west and Wrightsville to the east.

HANOVER

Located in southwestern York County, Hanover is the second largest urban community in York County. The land that now includes Hanover was known as Digges' Choice in 1727, when Irish nobleman John Digges purchased the land and German settlers began arriving. The first settlers arrived in the Hanover area around 1730, and by 1745 Richard McAllister owned the land that was to become the future borough. McAllister, who was Scots-Irish, had the area laid out in 1763, marking the beginning of McAllister's Town. The town was established to the southwest of the Pigeon Hills. Because the Monocacy Road, the primary route from central Pennsylvania to points in western Maryland and Virginia, passed through the area, McAllister's Town became a hub for goods and service for early travelers. The name of the town was later changed to Hanover, in honor of Hannover, Germany, an area from where many of the settlers came.

In late June 1863, the borough witnessed the first major battle on Union soil, the Battle of Hanover. The Union cavalry under General Judson Kilpatrick passed through town on the morning of June 30. As they slowly made their way through town, the Confederate cavalry under J.E.B. Stuart arrived and attacked the Union rear. The battle lasted several hours and was primarily fought within the borough. Viewed as a "draw" by most historians, the battle is significant in that it delayed Stuart's arrival in York, where he was to rendezvous with General Jubal Early. Stuart never met up with the general, however, and didn't reach Gettysburg until the end of the second day of fighting. The Battle of Hanover also marked the first battle for George Armstrong Custer after his promotion to general.

Hanover is laid out around a central square, appropriately called Centre Square, with five roads radiating from it. Many prominent buildings are located in and around the square, including one of the few Art Deco buildings in the borough, the 1930 Hanover Shoe building. The National

Register of Historic Places historic district was established in 1996 and today contains over three thousand contributing buildings. Approximately half of the buildings in town are from the Victorian era, with the most prominent styles being Queen Anne, Colonial Revival and what is deemed "vernacular"—that is, a simple local style prominent in the area.

Neas House

Hanover

The Neas House (or Nace House) is named for its first owner and first burgess of Hanover, George Neas. He was a writer and poet, but is perhaps better known for his roles in public life, serving as justice of the peace, in the Pennsylvania legislature from 1807 to 1810 and as postmaster of Hanover from 1799 to 1813. Neas also owned a tannery.

His striking home was constructed in 1795 and is a transitional Georgian-Federal house. Its formal design includes symmetrical façade, splayed lintels with keystones and double-end chimneys. A transom is located above the main entrance, while the foundation is constructed of fieldstone. Brickwork is Flemish bond. Most surviving eighteenth-century buildings in

York County are simple and vernacular in design, so the Neas House is an extremely important example of eighteenth-century architecture.

Conewago Chapel

Hanover

The Conewago Chapel is the only building featured in this book that is *not* located in York County. However, it is located just over the border in Adams County and was physically located in York County when it was originally constructed in 1787. In 1800, the County of Adams was formed from the County of York. The Basilica of the Sacred Heart of Jesus is noteworthy on a national level because it is the oldest stone Catholic church in the United States. This church, which replaced a 1741 log structure, served as the headquarters for Jesuit missionaries who fanned out through central and western Pennsylvania, western Maryland and the Shenandoah Valley in Virginia. A rectory adjoining the chapel was also constructed in the eighteenth century; however, it was greatly modified in subsequent years. The original roof of the brownstone chapel was timber framed. An eighty-foot spire was added in 1873, with the bell being placed in 1891.

Hanover Post Office

Hanover

The Hanover Post Office building is Hanover's best example of Italian Renaissance architecture. The post office opened in 1913 and is constructed of smooth-cut sandstone. Like the York Post Office, the building was

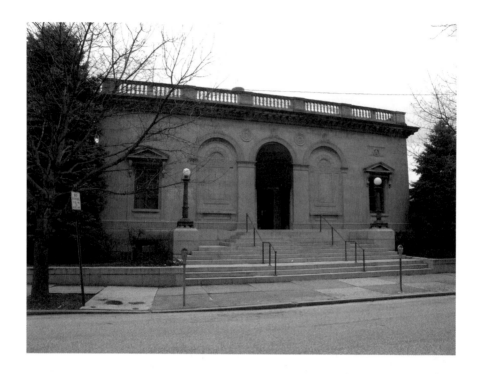

designed by James Knox Taylor, supervising architect of the Department of the Treasury from 1897 to 1912. Funding was obtained through an appropriation by Twentieth District Congressman Daniel F. Lafean, who used his success in obtaining the appropriations as a cornerstone of his reelection campaign.

This building is notable for its many features, including rosettes, balustrade, modillions and dentils under the roof eaves, arches, window pediments and more. To either side of the entrance are "blind arches," meaning that they are attached to the wall and are for decorative purposes only.

Young Memorial Library

2 Library Place, Hanover

Known originally as Young Memorial Library and later as Hanover Public Library, this building was constructed in 1911 and has a Beaux-Arts feel to it, though on a small scale. Stairs lead to the shallow entrance portico, flanked by two colossal columns with Corinthian capitals. A truncated hipped roof actually creates a French mansard appearance, while stone quoins, keystones and a balanced façade are all present. In 2003, construction

began on a large expansion project that retained the historic original building while adding new space in a large adjacent building. The expanded and remodeled library opened in 2006 as Guthrie Memorial Library.

Hanover Saving Fund Society

Carlisle Street, Hanover

Established in 1835, the Hanover Saving Fund Society was the second-oldest bank in York County. In 1907, the bank constructed this imposing building at a cost of approximately $100,000. The fifty- by one-hundred-foot building incorporates Barre Vermont granite on the exterior as well as mahogany and American Pavanaza marble on the interior.

The Neoclassical façade features four colossal Ionic columns, though the high-relief ornamentation adds an overall Beaux-Arts feel.

Peoples National Bank

Hanover

Peoples National Bank of Hanover was organized in 1892 and constructed this prominent building on Center Square in 1901. The construction cost was approximately $15,000. The eclectic façade combines Italian Renaissance features like rusticated first floor and distinct horizontal divisions, with Romanesque Revival elements such as arched windows and

corbel table. Perhaps most striking is the building's roofline, combining hipped and pyramidal roofs. Colossal columns with Scamozzi capitals are another notable feature.

In front of the building prominently sit two Civil War–era cannons, commemorating the Battle of Hanover fought in the streets of Hanover.

Emmanuel Reformed Church

124 Broadway, Hanover

The congregation of Emmanuel Reformed Church dates from the mid-eighteenth century and originally worshipped with the local Lutherans. In 1763, the congregation obtained land from Richard McAllister, founder of Hanover, for the purpose of constructing a church, parsonage, schoolhouse and graveyard. In 1766, a log church was constructed at 110 York Street. The building was later replaced with a brick structure. Reverend William Zieber led the church in the mid-1800s and also served as president of Hanover's Committee of Safety during the Civil War and Battle of Hanover. In 1856, a new church was constructed on Abbottstown Street, which is today known as Broadway Street.

The current church was dedicated in 1904. J.A. Dempwolf was the architect of the Late Gothic Revival building as well as a brick chapel constructed a year earlier to the rear of the property. It was built at a cost of $70,000. Notable features include a front façade of Avondale marble quarried near Philadelphia, towers with battlements and a large rose window.

Eichelberger High School

Hanover

This striking structure was built in 1896 as the Eichelberger Academy and was greatly altered and expanded in 1932. The Reinhardt Dempwolf–designed building was constructed by Abdiel Wirt Eichelberger at his own expense. He created a private institution to prepare young men and women for college. Eichelberger was a railroad tycoon, serving as president of the Hanover Branch Railroad Company, Bachman Valley, Berlin Branch and Baltimore & Harrisburg. He also served as president of Hanover Gas Company, organized the United Blues Rifle Company and commanded the Fourth Dragoons Cavalry Company. In 1900 he presented the building to Hanover Borough for use as a public high school.

The central portion of the building remains true to Dempwolf's design, though a number of alterations were made in the 1932 expansion. The

high-style Colonial Revival building employs piano nobile to focus attention above ground level. The Neoclassical portico is the most striking feature of the building and includes Ionic columns, dentilled pediment with bull's-eye window and rustication. Other features of the façade include splayed lintels with keystones, water table, belt course and Flemish bond brickwork. A cupola sits atop the hipped roof.

Sheppard and Myers Mansions

Hanover

Sometimes referred to as "the houses that shoes built," the twin Sheppard and Myers Mansions were the homes of Harper Donelson Sheppard and C.N. Myers, partners in the Hanover Shoe Company. The two men took over a floundering shoe factory in 1899 and reorganized the company. In 1900 they opened their first shoe store in York and by the early 1900s the company was producing five thousand pairs of shoes per week, growing to twenty-three retail stores in 1907. Philadelphia architect Herman Miller was hired in 1911 to design new homes, and the Myers Mansion (pictured) was constructed first, with the Sheppard Mansion completed in 1913. The

two gentlemen were prominent in other Hanover businesses, too, including Hanover General Hospital, the *Evening Sun* and Hanover Shoe Farms.

As is a popular theme with early twentieth-century mansions in York County, the homes combine Colonial Revival features with colossal Neoclassical porticos. The porticos feature Ionic capitals and balustrades. Other features of the homes include Palladian windows, quoins, splayed windows with keystones and hipped roofs.

WHY PRESERVATION
IS IMPORTANT

In its heyday, the 200 block of South Duke Street was an architectural delight. Standing side by side were two of the most significant buildings ever constructed in York County, both designed by York's greatest architect, J.A. Dempwolf. The York City Market was constructed in 1878 and designed in the High Victorian Gothic style of architecture. A clock tower reached the height of 140 feet, just 15 feet shy of the top of the main dome on the York County Court House. The building was demolished in 1963 to make way for a gas station. Its neighbor was the York Collegiate Institute, a beautiful Victorian Romanesque structure built in 1887 to replace the previous building, which had been destroyed by fire. It too would fall to the wrecking ball in the 1960s.

York is remarkably well preserved, yet some of the most significant buildings ever constructed are long gone. The York County Almshouse and Hospital perished, as did the prominent mansions at the intersection of Richland Avenue and West Market Street. The massive Springdale mansion on South George Street was demolished to make way for a medical center that was never built. And while a 1976 replica of the first York County Court House stands along West Market Street, the "real" one was demolished in 1841 to help traffic flow in Centre Square. That demolition was not without controversy, however: many local residents realized the significance of the building and fought to have it relocated and preserved. After all, it was in that building that the Second Continental Congress of the United States met for nine months in 1777–78.

Today, historic buildings are still being demolished. Sometimes the demolition is inevitable. The Lincoln Highway Garage was a landmark on the York County section of the Lincoln Highway that was demolished by a convenience store chain in 2004 to make way for a new store. The existing building, however, was in an advanced state of disrepair. Twenty-

The Victorian Romanesque York Collegiate Institute was constructed in 1887 from a design by J.A. Dempwolf.

Theodore Helb was a prominent businessman and owner of Keystone Brewing Company. His Queen Anne residence stood on West Market Street.

two buildings were razed to make way for Sovereign Bank Stadium along the Codorus Creek. All were contributing buildings to the York Historic District and were listed on the National Register of Historic Places. But the entire neighborhood was in a state of disrepair and sometimes economic development trumps historic preservation. The new stadium is certainly an asset for the community.

And what will become of the old York County Prison on Chestnut Street? The building itself is a fortress, but it has stood vacant since 1979. How feasible is it to attempt to adaptively reuse the building for another purpose? Furthermore, the neighborhood around the building has seen better days, making the prison even more unattractive to potential buyers.

So why should we care about preservation?

Before we can care about it, we must first define it. "Preservation" is both a catchall term as well as a specific approach to renovation. In general, a building can be considered "historic" if it is at least fifty years old. It doesn't have to be listed on a national, state or local register or be located in a historic district.

"Historic preservation" is a phrase often used to refer to renovation of a historic building. But there are also three "treatments" defined by the Secretary of the Interior's Standards for the Treatment of Historic Properties, the national guidelines for renovating historic buildings. Under the Standards, "preservation" specifically relates to retaining a building's historic features through conservation, maintenance and repair.

"Rehabilitation" is the second treatment, and it refers to retaining and repairing historic features, but with the understanding that due to deterioration, more latitude is allowed. Rehabilitation allows reinterpretation of space. Adaptive reuse is a phrase that describes renovating an existing building and adapting it for a new use other than for what it was originally constructed. When done within a historic building, it is a rehabilitation. The conversion of the 1898 York County Court House into a government office building is both an adaptive reuse and a rehabilitation.

The third treatment is "restoration," and involves retaining materials from a building's most significant time period while removing materials from other time periods. During the renovation of the William C. Goodridge Freedom House—an Underground Railroad Museum, a mid-twentieth-century addition was removed. This is an example of restoration.

There is a fourth treatment, known as "reconstruction," which involves re-creating a nonsurviving building using new materials. The catch, however, is that the historic building being reconstructed must be well documented through plans, photographs, etc. While the York County Colonial Court House is a replica, the designers had to make some educated guesses about its appearance, so it is not a reconstruction.

At its most basic, preservation is about connecting with the past. It has often been said that to understand where you are going, you have to first recognize where you have been. Historic buildings allow a community to embrace its past. While a few of the buildings featured in this guide are open to the public, most are privately owned. Many of the owners are passionate about preserving and restoring their buildings, which is of great benefit to the community. Unfortunately, many historic buildings don't experience TLC from their owners, and fall further into disrepair. Regardless of a building's condition, however, its mere existence can provide an education about the community of the past.

Historic buildings create a sense of place. Several years ago I had the opportunity to give a tour of York to an architect from Tampa. He stayed at the Yorktowne Hotel, and I showed him around the downtown as well as older, established neighborhoods like Springdale. I'll never forget a comment he made: "I wish Tampa was more like York." While Tampa is a vibrant, growing, modern community, this architect felt that Tampa lacked the sense of place that York espoused. Simply stated, historic buildings define communities. And it is not just the signature buildings: block after block of historic buildings create character and charm like no new development could ever hope to create. When Walt Disney World opened, it looked to establish main streets throughout the country as inspiration for its own Main Street. Fast-food chains and big box retailers create the antithesis of a sense of place. As Mark Twain stated in a 1900 toast to New York City, "We take stock of a city like we take stock of a man. The clothes or appearance are the externals by which we judge."

Preservation of historic buildings also promotes tourism. I recently came across a quote from Arthur Frommer, the tourism guru: "Tourism simply doesn't go to a city that has lost its soul." Historic towns like York have soul, and heart, because of a well-preserved building stock. The National Trust for Historic Places is a leading proponent of heritage tourism. Annually, it recognizes the "Dozen Distinctive Destinations"—cities and towns across the United States that offer authentic experiences, from attractive architecture to restored downtowns to abundant cultural activities. Much of York City's tourism product is based upon historic buildings, such as Golden Plough Tavern, General Horatio Gates House, Bobb Log House, Bonham House, Fire Museum of York County, Agricultural & Industrial Museum and the Colonial Court House replica.

Economics also play a role in preservation. In many cases it is cheaper to renovate an existing building than construct a new one. Furthermore, if the building is historic, the owner may be eligible for Rehabilitation Investment Tax Credits, commonly called Historic Tax Credits. This program encourages historic renovation by providing financial incentives. Historic preservation also improves the value of a property; several studies conducted throughout the country have found that properties located in a historic district appreciate at rates greater than the community as a whole. Purchasing a historic property is a wise investment.

Beyond a connection with the past, a sense of place, tourism opportunities and economics, a fifth benefit of historic preservation has recently come to the forefront: sustainability. Historic buildings are "green" because they are already built. A fancy new "green building" with all the latest features is still bad for the environment. One study concluded that it would take forty years of energy savings to recoup the energy used to construct a new green building. And if another building was torn down to make way for the green building, the energy payback is more like sixty-five years.

The concept of "embodied energy" has become a rallying cry of both preservationists and environmentalists. There is a lot of energy used to construct a building. First, raw materials must be mined, harvested, etc. Then they must be transported. Factories use tremendous amounts of energy for production, often giving off greenhouse gases. Perhaps a product can be totally manufactured in one factory, or maybe there are several factories involved with the process—meaning more transportation. Eventually, the product (such as a window) is finished. It is then trucked to a warehouse, or perhaps goes to a series of warehouses before it ends up on a construction site. Think of all the energy that is used along the way. Finally, there is the energy used to construct the building itself.

All this energy is now "embodied" within the building. If you take a downtown commercial building of about fifty thousand square feet, the embodied energy is the equivalent of approximately 640,000 gallons of gas! And if the building is demolished, all that energy is lost. Reconstructing a new building will emit the carbon dioxide equivalent of driving 2.8 million miles. Energy is a precious resource, and yet the Brookings Institute estimates that one-third of all buildings currently standing in the United States will be demolished by 2030. In the 1990s, over 740,000 homes constructed before 1920 were demolished.

Preservation is good for the environment. Renovating an existing building uses far less energy, and causes far less pollution, than constructing a new building. Historic buildings, contrary to popular belief, really are energy efficient. The perception of a "drafty old house" is simply that—a perception—and an inaccurate one at that. The General Services Administration, owner of nonmilitary Federal buildings, has found that utility costs for historic buildings are actually 27 percent lower than with modern buildings. Another study found that buildings constructed prior to 1920 are about as energy efficient as buildings constructed after 2000, with buildings constructed between 1920 and 2000 being less energy efficient. Simple solutions like storm windows, caulking, weather stripping and added insulation can make a historic building as energy efficient as a typical modern building. With all the benefits of historic preservation, it is still amazing that society has such a disposable mentality when it comes to buildings.

Imagine a world without historic buildings—one without the Parthenon in Greece or the Cathédrale Notre Dame de Paris in France or Mount Vernon in Virginia. Picture York County without the Golden Plough Tavern or Neas House or Warrington Meeting House. Now visualize York with the York City Market, York Collegiate Institute and countless other signature buildings still standing.

It's a nice picture, isn't it?

Fortunately, York County has a great local resource in Historic York, Inc. The nonprofit organization is dedicated to education and advocacy for historic buildings and properties, working with local residents and businesses to save treasures from the past. Karen Arnold, executive director of Historic York, Inc., sums up preservation this way: "Preservation is a true respect of past craftsmanship and knowledge that its permanence is worth keeping for future generations."

To know where we are headed, we must understand where we've been. Historic buildings are our collective past, and historic preservation allows us to retain history and a sense of place while providing an invaluable, sustainable resource for generations to come.

WORKS CONSULTED

Arnold, Karen. *National Register of Historic Places Nomination Form: Springdale Historic District*. York, PA: Historic York, Inc., 2001.

Baker, John Milnes, AIA. *American House Styles—A Concise Guide*. New York: W.W. Norton & Company, 1994.

Bentley, William S., and Melinda G. Higgins. *National Register of Historic Places Registration Form: Eichelberger High School*. York, PA: Historic York, Inc., 1995.

Berman, David M., and Sally McMurry. *National Register of Historic Places Inventory—Nomination Form: Laurel-Rex Fire Company House*. Harrisburg, PA: Office of Historic Preservation, 1976.

Blumenson, John J.G. *Identifying American Architecture, Revised Edition*. New York: W.W. Norton & Company, Inc., 1981.

Burden, Ernest. *Illustrated Dictionary of Architectural Preservation*. New York: McGraw-Hill, 2004.

———. *Illustrated Dictionary of Architecture—Second Edition*. New York: McGraw-Hill, 2002.

Butcher, Scott D. *Civil War Walking Tour of York, Pennsylvania*. York, PA: York County Heritage Trust, 2006.

———. *Postcard History Series: York*. Charleston, SC: Arcadia Publishing, 2005.

Carley, Rachel. *The Visual Dictionary of Domestic Architecture*. New York: Henry Holt and Company, LLC, 1994.

Curtis, Wayne. "A Cautionary Tale." *Preservation Magazine* (January/February 2008): 19–24.

Deardorff, Susan. *National Register of Historic Places Registration Form: York Central Market*. Harrisburg, PA: Pennsylvania Historical and Museum Commission, 1977.

Downing, A.J. *The Architecture of County Houses*. New York: Dover Publications, Inc., 1969.

Epler, Carole W. *National Register of Historic Places Registration Form: East York Historic District*. York, PA: Historic York, Inc., 1997.

Foster, Gerald. *American Houses: A Field Guide to the Architecture of the House*. New York: Houghton Mifflin Company, 2004.

Foust, Thomas, and William K. Watson. *National Register of Historic Places Nomination Form: Farmers Market*. York, PA: Office of City Planning, 1977.

Fredenburg, Harvey, and David Berman. *National Register of Historic Places Nomination Form: Conewago Chapel*. Harrisburg, PA: Pennsylvania Historical and Museum Commission, 1974.

Harris, Cyril M. *American Architecture: An Illustrated Encyclopedia*. New York: W.W. Norton & Company, 1998.

———. *Illustrated Dictionary of Historic Architecture*. New York: Dover Publications, Inc., 1977.

Higgins, Melinda G., and Thomas N. Shaffer. *National Register of Historic Places Registration Form: The Village of Muddy Creek Forks*. York, PA: Historic York, Inc., 1993.

Higgins, Mindy. *Historic Preservation Certification Application: Boxhill*. York, PA: Historic York, Inc., 1998.

Historic York, Inc. *Downtown York Design Guide*. York, PA: 1981.

————. *National Register of Historic Places Inventory—Nomination Form: Willis House*. York, PA: Historic York, Inc., 1979.

Historical Society of York County. *Architecture in York County*. York, PA: Historical Society of York County, 1979.

Howe, Jeffery. *Houses of Worship—An Identification Guide to the History and Styles of American Religious Architecture*. San Diego, CA: Thunder Bay Press, 2003.

————. *The Houses We Live In—An Identification Guide to the History and Style of American Domestic Architecture*. San Diego, CA: Thunder Bay Press, 2002.

Jensen, Lisa. *National Register of Historic Places Inventory—Nomination Form: Northwest Historic District*. York, PA: Historic York, Inc., 1983.

Kearney, Carol A. *National Register of Historic Places Inventory—Nomination Form: The Nook, Francis Farquhar House*. York, PA: Carol A. Kearney, 1979.

Klein, Mailyn, and David P. Fogle. *Clues to American Architecture*. Montgomery, AL: Starhill Press, 1986.

McAlester, Virginia, and Lee McAlester. *A Field Guide to American Houses*. New York: Alfred Knopf, 1995.

McClure, James. *Never to be Forgotten*. York, PA: York Daily Record, 1999.

McMurray, Sally. *National Register of Historic Places Nomination Form: Guinston United Presbyterian Church*. Harrisburg: Pennsylvania Historical & Museum Commission, 1974.

Mosely, Thresa M., and R. Stefan Klosowski. *National Register of Historic Places Inventory—Nomination Form: Spring Grove Borough Historic District*. York, PA: Historic York, Inc., 1983.

Peckham, Betty. *The Story of a Dynamic Community: York, Pennsylvania*. York, PA: York County Chamber of Commerce, 1945.

————. *York Pennsylvania: A Dynamic Community Forges Ahead*. York, PA: York County Chamber of Commerce, 1957.

Pennsylvania Register of Historic Sites and Landmarks. *National Register of Historic Places Nomination Form: George Nace (Neas) Home.* Harrisburg: Pennsylvania Historical and Museum Commission, 1971.

Pettit, N. Allan, III. *York City: 250 Years.* York, PA: Campbell, Harrington & Brear, Inc., 1991.

Poppeliers, John C., et al. *What Style Is It? A Guide to American Architecture.* New York: John Wiley & Sons, Inc., 1983.

Prowell, George R. *History of York County, Pennsylvania.* Chicago: J.H. Beers & Co., 1907.

Raid, B. *National Register of Historic Places Nomination Form: Fairmount Historic District.* York, PA: Historic York, Inc., 1999.

————. *National Register of Historic Places Nomination Form: Hanover Historic District.* York, PA: Historic York, Inc., 1996.

Reed, Diane B. *National Register of Historic Places Nomination Form: Codorus Forge & Furnace Historic District.* Harrisburg: Pennsylvania Historic and Museum Commission, 1991.

Remy, Patricia A. *Pennsylvania Historic Resource Form: Old Columbia-Wrightsville Bridge.* PennDOT, 1982.

Rifkind, Carole. *A Field Guide to American Architecture.* New York: Penguin Group, 1980.

Rohrbeck, Benson. *York County Trolleys: An Illustrated History of the Street Railway in York County, Penn.* West Chester, PA: Ben Rohrbeck Traction Publications, 1978.

Roman, Elizabeth L. *National Register of Historic Places Registration Form: Red Lion Borough Historic District.* York, PA: Historic York, Inc., 2000.

Rudisill, James. *York Since 1741.* York, PA: York Graphic Services, 1991.

Rypkema, Donovan D. "Economics, Sustainability, and Historic Preservation." *Forum Journal* (Winter 2006).

Schaefer, Thomas N. *National Register of Historic Places Nomination Form: Hanover Junction Rail Station*. York, PA: Historic York, Inc., 1982.

Schein, John R., Jr., and David C. Stacks. *National Register of Historic Places Nomination Form: York Historic District*. York, PA: Historic York, Inc., 197?.

Shaffer, Thomas N. *National Register of Historic Places Registration Form: Howard Tunnel, Northern Central Railway*. York, PA: Historic York, Inc., 1992.

Sheets, Georg R. *Made in York: A Survey of the Agricultural and Industrial Heritage of York County, Pennsylvania*. York, PA: Agricultural and Industrial Museum of York County, 1991.

————. *To the Setting of the Sun: The Story of York*. Windsor, PA: Windsor Publications, 1981.

Springettsbury Township Centenial Committee. *Springettsbury Township Centennial, 1891–1991*. York, PA: Anstadt Printing Craftsmen, Inc., 1991.

Taub, Lynn Smolens. *Greater York in Action*. York, PA: York Area Chamber of Commerce, 1968.

Van Sweden, Bryan, and Thomas N. Shaffer. *National Register of Historic Places Registration Form: United States Post Office, Hanover*. York, PA: Historic York, Inc., 1992.

Vogden, Grant H., and Susan M. Zacher. *National Register of Historic Places Nomination Form: Wallace-Cross Mill*. York/Harrisburg, PA: York County Board of Parks & Recreation/P.H.M.C., 1976.

Walker, Lester. *American Homes—An Illustrated Encyclopedia of Domestic Architecture*. New York: Black Dog & Leventhal Publishers, 1981.

Wallick, P.L. *National Register of Historic Places Nomination Form: Dritt Mansion*. Harrisburg: Pennsylvania Historical and Museum Commission, 1977.

Watson, William K. *National Register of Historic Places Nomination Form: Warrington Meetinghouse*. Harrisburg: Pennsylvania Historical and Museum Commission, 1974.

Whiffen, Marcus. *American Architecture Since 1780—A Guide to the Styles*. Revised Edition. Cambridge, MA: MIT Press, 1999.

York, PA Office of City Planning. *York: Historic Buildings and Plan for Preservation*. York, PA: 1982.

Pamphlets and Unpublished Works

Butcher, Scott D. "Architecture: York—A Guide to York's Architectural Styles." York, PA: Unpublished, 1991.

"First Annual York City Church Open House." Saturday, December 13, 2003.

"House Tour 2000: Elmwood." Historic York, Inc., 2000.

"House Tour 2001: Northwest Area." Historic York, Inc., 2001.

"House Tour 2002: Grantley Hills." Historic York, Inc., 2002.

"How to Complete the Pennsylvania Historic Resource Survey Form." Bureau for Historic Preservation, Pennsylvania Historical and Museum Commission. Harrisburg, 1991 (Revised 2001).

"Preservation Leadership Training." National Trust for Historic Preservation, 2003.

"Rivertownes PA USA, Located on the Scenic Susquehanna River." Columbia, PA: Rivertownes PA USA.

"The Story Behind the Elmwood Mansion." Memorial Hospital, 2002.

"Walking Tour." York County Heritage Trust.

York Historic District Revised Resource Inventory, 2001–02.

"York's Architecture and the Dempwolf Influence."

Online Sources

Architectural Encyclopedia: Archpedia. http://www.archpedia.com.

Buffalo as an Architectural Museum. http://www.buffaloah.com/a/bamname.html.

"Central Market House—Market History," 2007. http://www.centralmarkethouse.com/market_history.html.

A Digital Archive of American Architecture. http://www.bc.edu/bc_org/avp/cas/fnart/fa267/default.html.

Encyclopedia Britannica Online. http://www.britannica.com.

"Existing Railroad Structures in York County," 2004. www.trainweb.org/rrofyork/sta.htm.

"History of the Sheppard Mansion," 2004. www.sheppardmansion.com/mansion_history.htm.

Moe, Richard. "Sustainable Stewardship: Historic Preservation's Essential Role in Fighting Climate Change." http://www.preservationnation.org/about-us/press-room/press-releases/2007/scully-prize-speech-sustainability.html. 2007.

National Register of Historic Places. http://www.nationalregisterofhistoricplaces.com.

Pennsylvania's Historic Architecture & Archaeology. http://www.arch.state.pa.us.

"Strand-Capitol Performing Arts Center History," 2004. http://www.strandcapitol.org/aboutus/.

Virtual York: A Journey Through History. http://www.virtualyork.com.

ABOUT THE AUTHOR

S cott D. Butcher is a lifelong resident of York County and an active participant in the community, having served on the boards of directors for Main Street York, York County Convention and Visitors Bureau and Leadership York. He has also served on the board of directors for Historic York, Inc., a nonprofit organization that provides historic preservation consulting, education and advocacy services. Scott regularly leads walking tours of downtown York and is the author of numerous local history books, including *Postcard History Series: York*, *Civil War Walking Tour of York, Pennsylvania* and *York: America's Historic Crossroads*. He has also written extensively about York and York County for visitors' guides, relocation guides, architectural features and websites. He has served as a living history volunteer with the York County Heritage Trust, volunteer with the William Goodridge Freedom House (an Underground Railroad Museum task force) and was instrumental in creating several local events, including Patriot Days: Prelude to Gettysburg, York Pear Blossom Festival and Downtown York Holiday Open House. Scott is an avid photographer and has also spent over eighteen years as a marketing professional with a regional architectural and engineering firm. Visit Scott online at www.scottbutcher.com or e-mail him at sbutcher@yorklinks.net.

Visit us at
www.historypress.net